THE STATE

ITS HISTORY AND DEVELOPMENT VIEWED SOCIOLOGICALLY

By

FRANZ OPPENHEIMER, M. D., Ph. D.

Privat Docent of Political Sciences in the
University of Berlin

AUTHORIZED TRANSLATION

By

JOHN M. GITTERMAN, Ph. D., LL. B.

(Of the New York County Bar)

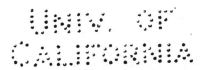

INDIANAPOLIS
THE BOBBS-MERRILL COMPANY
PUBLISHERS

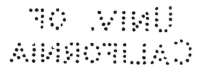
PRESS OF
BRAUNWORTH & CO.
BOOKBINDERS AND PRINTERS
BROOKLYN, N. Y.

PREFACE

THE STATE first appeared in Germany in 1908. Since then a Hungarian edition has been published, a French translation has been made, and Roumanian and Italian translations are in course of preparation.

Perhaps it is not surprising that the faculties of the great German universities maintained complete silence about this work, just as they had done in the case of most of the author's other books, while in the meantime they put the stamp of their highest approval on less worthy publications. But despite their opposition no less an authority than Herr Adolph Wagner, Dean of the University of Berlin and foremost among German political economists, in his *Handwörterbuch der Staatswissenschaften*, in the course of the paper entitled "Der Staat in Nationalökonomischer Hinsicht," pronounced THE STATE to be the most important work of its kind ever published.

An epitome of Oppenheimer's political and historical philosophy is contained in THE STATE. One may say, indeed, that it furnishes a perspective of his universal philosophy, seen *sub specie æternitatis*, or, as Oppenheimer himself puts it, seen from a so-called cosmic distance in which the details disappear and only the movement of the mass, struggling developing humanity, re-

iii

mains visible. Half of the present volume contains the author's interpretation of sociology—an integration of political and historical philosophy on the one hand, with economic philosophy on the other. In a book published in 1910 under the title, *Theorie der Reinen und Politischen Okonomie: Ein Lehr- und Lesebuch für Studierende und Gebildete,* we find worked out some of the economic questions treated of in THE STATE.

As a result of his work the author has acquired a great following in the German universities, and this may account for the fact that a number of years ago he was installed as a docent of economy and sociology in the University of Berlin.

Doctor Oppenheimer believes that the future progress of nations will be in the direction pointed out by liberal socialism. He contends that we can and probably will establish a society free from all monopolistic tendencies by unfettering competition, which to-day is far from free.

Competition is now enslaved because in our present society there exists a powerful class monopoly, not created through economic differentiation, as up to this time students of the question have believed, but through political power. This class monopoly stands between the masses and the land, and so a laboring class is established which may be influenced by the upper classes because it is not in control of the means of production necessary for carrying on its work in its own interest. This land obstacle is known legally as *Grossgrundeigentum*—the personal possession of unlimited land holdings. According to Oppenheimer the right to hold more land than one through his own efforts and the efforts of his family can properly work has existed only because of political control, can not exist without political control, and is the one explanation for the formation of all monopolies in human society, by which is meant ground rents and profits to capital. Doctor Oppenheimer has proved his theory through a new and very original analysis of the whole conception of monopolies.

If the transition is not too violent it may be better to add here, so as to avoid possible confusion, an explanation of the notes in this volume. All foot-notes are referred to in the text by means of asterisks (*), while those notes which will be found gathered together at the end of the text are referred to by means of Arabic numerals.

—*The Translator*

Washington, October 3, 1913.

CONTENTS

THE STATE

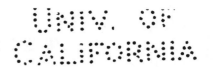

THE STATE

CHAPTER I

THEORIES OF THE STATE

THIS treatise regards the State from the sociological standpoint only, not from the juristic—sociology, as I understand the word, being both a philosophy of history and a theory of economics. Our object is to trace the development of the State from its socio-psychological genesis up to its modern constitutional form; after that, we shall endeavor to present a well-founded prognosis concerning its future development. Since we shall trace only the State's inner, essential being, we need not concern ourselves with the external forms of law under which its international and intra-national life is assumed. This treatise, in short, is a contribution to the philosophy of State development; but only in so far as the law of development here traced from its generic form affects also the social problems common to forms of the modern State.

With this limitation of treatment in mind, we may at the outset dismiss all received doctrines of public law. Even a cursory examination of conventional theories of the State is sufficient to show that they furnish no explanation of its genesis, essence and purpose. These theories represent all possible shadings between all imaginable extremes. Rousseau derives the State from a social contract, while Carey ascribes its origin to a band of robbers. Plato and the followers of Karl Marx endow the State with omnipotence, making it the absolute lord over the citizen in all political and economic matters; while Plato even goes so far as to wish the State to regulate sexual relations. The Manchester school, on the other hand, going to the opposite extreme of liberalism, would have the State exercise only needful police functions, and would thus logically have as a result a scientific anarchism which must utterly exterminate the State. From these various and conflicting views, it is impossible either to establish a fixed principle, or to formulate a satisfactory concept of the real essence of the State.

This irreconcilable conflict of theories is easily explained by the fact that none of the conventional theories treats the State from the sociological view-point. Nevertheless, the State is a phenomenon common to all history, and its essential nature can only be made plain by an adequate and comprehensive study of universal history. Except in the field of sociology, the king's highway of science, no treatment of the State has heretofore taken this path. All previous theories of the State have been class theories. To anticipate somewhat the outcome of our researches, every State has been and is a class State, and every theory of the State has been and is a class theory.

A class theory is, however, of necessity, not the result of investigation and reason, but a by-product of desires and will. Its arguments are used, not to establish truth, but as weapons in the contest for material interests. The result, therefore, is not science, but nescience. By understanding the State, we may indeed recognize the essence of theories concerning the State. But the converse is not true. An understanding of theories about the State will give us no clue to its essence.

The following may be stated as a ruling concept, especially prevalent in university teaching, of the origin and essence of the State. It represents a view which, in spite of manifold attacks, is still affirmed.

It is maintained that the State ganization of human community originates by reason of a social instinct planted in men by nature (Stoic Doctrine); or else is brought about by an irresistible impulse to end the "war of all against all," and to coerce the savage, who opposes organized effort, to a peaceable community life in place of the anti-social struggle in which all budding shoots of advancement are destroyed (Epicurean Doctrine). These two apparently irreconcilable concepts were fused by the intermediation of mediæval philosophy. This, founded on theologic reasoning and belief in the Bible, developed the opinion that man, originally and by nature a social creature, is, through original sin, the fratricide of Cain and the transgression at the tower of Babel, divided into innumerable tribes, which fight to the hilt, until they unite peaceably as a State.

This view is utterly untenable. It confuses the logical concept of a class with some subordinate species thereof. Granted that the State is *one* form of organized political cohesion, it is also to be remembered that it is a form having *specific* characteristics. Every state in history was or is a *state of classes*, a polity of superior and inferior social groups, based upon distinctions either of rank or of property. This phenomenon must, then, be called the "State." With it alone history occupies itself.

We should, therefore, be justified in designating every other form of political organization by the same term, without further differentiation, had there never existed any other than a class-state, or were it the only conceivable form. At least, proof might properly be called for, to show that each conceivable political organization, even though originally it did not represent a polity of superior and inferior social and economic classes, since it is of necessity subject to inherent laws of development, must in the end be resolved into the specific class form of history. Were such proof forthcoming, it would offer in fact only one form of political amalgamation, calling in turn for differentiation at various stages of development, viz., the preparatory stage, when class distinction does not exist, and the stage of maturity, when it is fully developed.

Former students of the philosophy of the State were dimly aware of this problem. And they tried to adduce the required proof, that because of inherent tendencies of development, every human political organization must gradually become a class-state. Philosophers of the canon law handed this theory down to philosophers of the law of nature. From these, through the mediation of Rousseau, it became a part of the teachings of the economists; and even to this day it rules their views and diverts them from the facts.

This assumed proof is based upon the concept of a "primitive accumulation," or an original store of wealth, in lands and in movable property, brought about by means of purely economic forces; a doctrine justly derided by Karl Marx as a "fairy tale." Its scheme of reasoning approximates this:

Somewhere, in some far-stretching, fertile country, a number of free men, of equal status, form a union for mutual protection. Gradually they differentiate into property classes. Those best endowed with strength, wisdom, capacity for saving, industry and caution, slowly acquire a basic amount of real or movable property; while the stupid and less efficient, and those given to carelessness and waste, remain without possessions. The well-to-do lend their productive property to the less well-off in return for tribute, either ground-rent or profit, and become thereby con-

tinually richer, while the others alwr.ys remain
poor. These differences in possession gradually develop social class distinctions; since
everywhere the rich have preference, while
they alone have the time and the means to devote to public affairs and to turn the laws administered by them to their own advantage.
Thus, in time, there develops a ruling and
property-owning estate, and a proletariate, a
class without property. The primitive state
of free and equal fellows becomes a class-state,
by an inherent law of development, because in
every conceivable mass of men there are, as
may readily be seen, strong and weak, clever
and foolish, cautious and wasteful ones.

This seems quite plausible, and it coincides
with the experience of our daily life. It is not
at all unusual to see an especially gifted member of the lower class rise from his former surroundings, and even attain a leading position
in the upper class; or conversely, to see some
spendthrift or weaker member of the higher
group "lose his class" and drop into the
proletariate.

And yet this entire theory is utterly mistaken; it is a "fairy tale," or it is a class theory used to justify the privileges of the upper classes. The class-state never originated in this fashion, and never could have so originated. History shows that it did not; and economics shows deductively, with a testimony absolute, mathematical and binding, that it could not. A simple problem in elementary arithmetic shows that the assumption of an original accumulation is totally erroneous, and has nothing to do with the development of the class-state.

The proof is as follows: All teachers of natural law, etc., have unanimously declared that the differentiation into income-receiving classes and propertyless classes can only take place when all fertile lands have been occupied. For so long as man has ample opportunity to take up unoccupied land, "no one," says Turgot, "would think of entering the service of another;" we may add, "at least for wages, which are not apt to be higher than the earnings of an independent peasant working an unmortgaged and sufficiently large property;" while mortgaging is not possible as long as land is yet free for the working or taking, as free as air and water. Matter that is obtainable for the taking has no value that enables it to be pledged, since no one loans on things that can be had for nothing.

The philosophers of natural law, then, assumed that complete occupancy of the ground must have occurred quite early, because of the natural increase of an originally small population. They were under the impression that at their time, in the eighteenth century, it had taken place many centuries previous, and they naïvely deduced the existing class aggroupment from the assumed conditions of that long-past point of time. It never entered their heads to work out their problem; and with few exceptions their error has been copied by sociologists, historians and economists. It is only quite recently that my figures were worked out, and they are truly astounding.*

* Franz Oppenheimer, *Theorie der Reinen und Politischen Œkonomie*. Berlin, 1912.—*Translator*.

We can determine with approximate accuracy the amount of land of average fertility in the temperate zone, and also what amount is sufficient to enable a family of peasants to exist comfortably, or how much such a family can work with its own forces, without engaging outside help or permanent farm servants. At the time of the migration of the barbarians (350 to 750 A. D.), the lot of each able-bodied man was about thirty morgen (equal to twenty acres) on average lands, on very good ground only ten to fifteen morgen (equal to seven or ten acres), four morgen being equal to one hectare. Of this land, at least a third, and sometimes a half, was left uncultivated each year. The remainder of the fifteen to twenty morgen sufficed to feed and fatten into giants the immense families of these child-producing Germans, and this in spite of the primitive technique, whereby at least half the productive capacity of a day was lost. Let us assume that, in these modern times, thirty morgen (equal to twenty acres) for the average peasant suffices to support a family.

We have then assumed a block of land sufficiently large to meet any objection. Modern
Germany, populated as it is, contains an agricultural area of thirty-four million hectares
(equal to eighty-four million, fifteen thousand,
four hundred and eighty acres). The agricultural population, including farm laborers and
their families, amounts to seventeen million;
so that, assuming five persons to a family and
an equal division of the farm lands, each
family would have ten hectares (equal to
twenty-five acres). In other words, not even
in the Germany of our own day would the
point have been reached where, according to
the theories of the adherents of natural law,
differentiation into classes would begin.

Apply the same process to countries less
densely settled, such, for example, as the Dan-
ube States, Turkey, Hungary and Russia, and
still more astounding results will appear. As
a matter of fact, there are still on the earth's
surface, seventy-three billion, two hundred
million hectares (equal to one hundred eighty
billion, eight hundred eighty million and four

hundred sixteen thousand acres) ; dividing into
the first amount the number of human beings
of all professions whatever, viz., one billion,
eight hundred million, every family of five
persons could possess about thirty morgen
(equal to eighteen and a half acres), *and still
leave about two-thirds of the planet unoccupied.*

If, therefore, purely economic causes are
ever to bring about a differentiation into
classes by the growth of a propertyless laboring class, the time has not yet arrived; and
the critical point at which ownership of land
will cause a natural scarcity is thrust into the
dim future—if indeed it ever can arrive.

As a matter of fact, however, for centuries
past, in all parts of the world, we have had a
class-state, with possessing classes on top and
a propertyless laboring class at the bottom,
even when population was much less dense
than it is to-day. Now it is true that the class-
state can arise only where all fertile acreage
.has been *occupied* completely; and since I have
shown that even at the present time, all the

ground is not occupied economically, this must mean that it has been preëmpted politically. Since land could not have acquired "natural scarcity," the scarcity must have been "legal." This means that the land has been preëmpted by a ruling class against its subject class, and settlement prevented. Therefore the State, as a class-state, can have originated in no other way than through conquest and subjugation.

This view, the so-called "sociologic idea of the state," as the following will show, is supported in ample manner by well-known historical facts. And yet most modern historians have rejected it, holding that both groups, amalgamated by · war into one State, before that time had, each for itself formed a "State." As there is no method of obtaining historical proof to the contrary, since the beginnings of human history are unknown, we should arrive at a verdict of "not proven," were it not that; deductively, there is the absolute certainty that the State, as history shows it, the class-state, could not have come about except through warlike subjugation. The mass µ evidence shows that our simple calculation excludes any other result.

THE SOCIOLOGICAL IDEA OF THE STATE

To the originally, purely sociological, idea of the State, I have added the economic phase and formulated it as follows:

What, then, is the State as a sociological concept? The State, completely in its genesis, essentially and almost completely during the first stages of its existence, is a social institution, forced by a victorious group of men on a defeated group, with the sole purpose of regulating the domin of the victorious group over the vanquished, and securing itself against revolt from within and attacks from abroad. Teleologically, this dominion had no other purpose than the economic exploitation of the vanquished by the victors.

No primitive state known to history originated in any other manner.[1] Wherever a reliable tradition reports otherwise, either it concerns the amalgamation of two fully developed primitive states into one body of more complete organization; or else it is an adaptation to men of the fable of the sheep which made a bear their king in order to be protected against the wolf. But even in this latter case, the form and content of the State became precisely the same as in those states where nothing intervened, and which became immediately "wolf states."

The little history learned in our school-days suffices to prove this generic doctrine. Everywhere we find some warlike tribe of wild men breaking through the boundaries of some less warlike people, settling down as nobility and founding its State. In Mesopotamia, wave follows wave, state follows state—Babylonians, Amoritans, Assyrians, Arabs, Medes, Persians, Macedonians, Parthians, Mongols, Seldshuks, Tartars, Turks; on the Nile, Hyksos, Nubians, Persians, Greeks, Romans, Arabs, Turks; in Greece, the Doric States are typical examples; in Italy, Romans, Ostrogoths, Lombards, Franks, Germans; in Spain, Carthaginians, Visigoths, Arabs; in Gaul, Romans, Franks, Burgundians, Normans; in

Britain, Saxons, Normans. In India wave
upon wave of wild warlike clans has flooded
over the country even to the islands of the Indian Ocean. So also is it with China. In the
European colonies, we find the selfsame type,
wherever a settled element of the population
has been found, as for example, in South
America and Mexico. Where that element is
lacking, where only roving huntsmen are
found, who may be exterminated but not subjugated, the conquerors resort to the device of
importing from afar masses of men to be exploited, to be subject perpetually to forced
labor, and thus the slave trade arises.

An apparent exception is found only in
those European colonies in which it is forbidden to replace the lack of a domiciled indige-
nous population by the importation of slaves.
One of these colonies, the United States of
America, is among the most powerful state-
formations in all history. The exception
there found is to be explained by this, that the
mass of men to be exploited and worked without cessation *imports itself*, by emigration in

great hordes from primitive states or from those in higher stages of development in which exploitation has become unbearable, while liberty of movement has been attained. In this case, one may speak of an infection from afar with "statehood" brought in by the infected of foreign lands. Where, however, in such colonies, immigration is very limited, either because of excessive distances and the consequent high charges for moving from home, or because of regulations limiting the immigration, we perceive an approximation to the final end of the development of the State, which we nowadays recognize as the necessary outcome and finale, but for which we have not yet found a scientific terminology. Here again, in the dialectic development, a change in the quantity is bound up with a change of the quality. The old form is filled with new contents. We still find a "State" in so far as it represents the tense regulation, secured by external force, whereby is secured the social living together of large bodies of men; but it is no longer the "State" in its older sense. It is no longer the instrument of political domination and economic exploitation of one social group by another; it is no longer a "State of Classes." It rather resembles a condition which appears to have come about through a "social contract." This stage is approached by the Australian Colonies, excepting Queensland, which after the feudal manner still exploits the half enslaved Kanakas.   It is almost attained in New Zealand.

So long as there is no general assent as to the origin and essence of states historically known or as to the sociological meaning of the word "State," it would be futile to attempt to force into use a new name for these most advanced commonwealths. They will continue to be called "states" in spite of all protests, especially because of the pleasure of using confusing concepts. For the purpose of this study, however, we propose to employ a new concept, a different verbal lever, and shall speak of the result of the new process as a "Freemen's Citizenship."

This summary survey of the states of the

past and present should, if space permitted, be supplemented by an examination of the facts offered by the study of races, and of those states which are not treated in our falsely called "Universal History." On this point, the assurance may be accepted that here again our general rule is valid without exception. Everywhere, whether in the Malay Archipelago, or in the "great sociological laboratory of Africa," at all places on this planet where the development of tribes has at all attained a higher form, the State grew from the subjugation of one group of men by another. Its basic justification, its raison d'être, was and is the economic exploitation of those subjugated.

The summary review thus far made may serve as proof of the basic premise of this sketch. The pathfinder, to whom, before all others, we are indebted for this line of investigation is Professor Ludwig Gumplowicz of Graz, jurist and sociologist, who crowned a brave life by a brave self-chosen death. We can, then, in sharp outlines, follow in the sufferings of humanity the path which the State has pursued in its progress through the ages. This we propose now to trace from the primitive state founded on conquest to the "freemen's citizenship."

[Class-State oRiginated through conquest of subjugation.]

CHAPTER II

THE GENESIS OF THE STATE

ONE single force impels all life; one force developed it, from the single cell, the particle of albumen floating about in the warm ocean of prehistoric time, up to the vertebrates, and then to man. This one force, according to Lippert, is the tendency to provide for life, bifurcated into "hunger and love." With man, however, philosophy also enters into the play of these forces, in order hereafter, together with "hunger and love, to hold together the structure of the world of men." To be sure, this philosophy, this "idea" of Schopenhauer's, is at its source nothing else than a creature of the provision for life called by him "will." It is an organ of orientation in the world, an arm in the struggle for existence. Yet in spite of this we shall come to know the (desire for caus ation as a self-acting force, and of social facts as coöperators in the sociological process of development.) In the beginning of human society, and as it gradually develops, this tendency pushes itself forward in various bizarre ideas called "superstition." These are based on purely logical conclusions from incomplete observations concerning air and water, earth and fire, animals and plants, which seem endowed with a throng of spirits both kindly and malevolent. One may say that in the most recent modern times, at a stage attained only by very few races, there arises also the younger daughter of the desire for causation, namely science, as a logical result of complete observation of facts; science, now required to exterminate widely branched-out superstition, which, with innumerable threads, has rooted itself in the very soul of mankind.

But, however powerfully, especially in the moment of "ecstasy," [2] superstition may have influenced history, however powerfully, even in ordinary times, it may have coöperated in the development of human communal life, the prin-

cipal force of development is still to be found
in the necessities of life, which force man to
acquire for himself and for his family nourishment, clothing and housing. This remains,
therefore, the "economic" impulse. A sociological—and that means a socio-psychological
—investigation of the development of history
can, therefore, not progress otherwise than by
following out the methods by which economic
needs have been satisfied in their gradual un-
folding, and by taking heed of the influences of
the causation impulse at its proper place.

(a) POLITICAL AND ECONOMIC MEANS

There are two fundamentally opposed
means whereby man, requiring sustenance, is
impelled to obtain the necessary means for sat-
isfying his desires. These are work and robbery, one's own labor and the forcible appropriation of the labor of others. Robbery!
Forcible appropriation! These words convey
to us ideas of crime and the penitentiary, since
we are the contemporaries of a developed civi-

lization, specifically based on the inviolability
of property.   And this tang is not lost when
we are convinced that land and sea robbery is
the primitive relation of life, just as the warriors' trade—which also for a long time is only
organized mass robbery—constitutes the most
respected of occupations.   Both because of
this, and also on account of the need of having,
in the further development of this study, terse,
clear, sharply opposing terms for these very
important contrasts, I propose in the following
discussion to call 'one's own labor and the
equivalent exchange of one's own labor for the
labor of others, the "economic means" for the
satisfaction of needs, while the unrequited appropriation of the labor of others will be called
the "political means."

The idea is not altogether new; philosophers
of history have at all times found this contradiction and have tried to formulate it.   But no
one of these formulæ has carried the premise to
its complete logical end.   At no place is it
clearly shown that the contradiction consists

only in the *means* by which the *identical purpose,* the acquisition of economic objects of consumption, is to be obtained. Yet this is the critical point of the reasoning. In the case of a thinker of the rank of Karl Marx, one may observe what confusion is brought about when economic purpose and economic means are not strictly differentiated. All those errors, which in the end led Marx's splendid theory so far away from truth, were grounded in the lack of clear differentiation between the means of economic satisfaction of needs and its end. This led him to designate slavery as an "economic category," and force as an "economic force"— half truths which are far more dangerous than total untruths, since their discovery is more difficult, and false conclusions from them are inevitable.

On the other hand, our own sharp differentiation between the two means toward the same end, will help us to avoid any such confusion. This will be our key to an understanding of the development, the essence, and the purpose of the State; and since all universal history heretofore has been only the history of states, to an understanding of universal history as well. All world history, from primitive times up to our own civilization, presents a single phase, a contest namely between the economic and the political means; and it can present only this phase until we have achieved free citizenship.

(b) PEOPLES WITHOUT A STATE: HUNTSMEN
AND GRUBBERS

The state is an organization of the political means. No state, therefore, can come into being until the economic means has created a definite number of objects for the satisfaction of needs, which objects may be taken away or appropriated by warlike robbery. For that reason, primitive huntsmen are without a state; and even the more highly developed huntsmen become parts of a state structure only when they find in their neighborhood an evolved economic organization which they can subjugate. But primitive huntsmen live in practical anarchy.

Grosse says concerning primitive huntsmen in general:

"There are no essential differences of fortune among them, and thus a principal source for the origin of differences in station is lacking. Generally, all grown men within the tribe enjoy equal rights. The older men, thanks to their greater experience, have a certain authority; but no one feels himself bound to render them obedience. Where in some cases chiefs are recognized—as with the Botokude, the Central Californians, the Wedda and the Mincopie—their power is extremely limited. The chieftain has no means of enforcing his wishes against the will of the rest. Most tribes of hunters, however, have no chieftain. The entire society of the males still forms a homogeneous undifferentiated mass, in which only those individuals achieve prominence who are believed to possess magical powers." [3]

Here, then, there scarcely exists a spark of "statehood," even in the sense of ordinary theories of the state, still less in the sense of the correct "sociologic idea of the state."

The social structure of primitive peasants has hardly more resemblance to a state than has the horde of huntsmen. Where the peasant, working the ground with a grub, is living in liberty, there is as yet no "state." The plow is always the mark of a higher economic condition which occurs only in a state; that is to say, in a system of plantation work carried on by subjugated servants.[4] The grubbers live isolated from one another, scattered over the country in separated curtilages, perhaps in villages, split up because of quarrels about district or farm boundaries. In the best cases, they live in feebly organized associations, bound together by oath, attached only loosely by the tie which the consciousness of the same descent and speech and the same belief imposes upon them. They unite perhaps once a year in the common celebration of renowned ancestors or of the tribal god. There is no ruling authority over the whole mass; the various chieftains of a village, or possibly of a district, may have more or less influence in their circumscribed spheres, this depending usually upon their personal qualities, and especially upon the magical powers attributed to them. Cunow describes the Peruvian peasants before the incursion of the Incas as follows: "An unregulated living side by side of many independent, mutually warring tribes, who again were split up into more or less autonomous territorial unions, held together by ties of kinship." [5] One may say that all the primitive peasants of the old and new world were of this type.

In such a state of society, it is hardly conceivable that a warlike organization could come about for purposes of attack. It is sufficiently difficult to mobilize the clan, or still more the tribe, for common defense. The peasant is always lacking in mobility. He is as attached to the ground as the plants he cultivates. As a matter of fact, the working of his field makes him "bound to the soil" (*glebæ adscriptus*), even though, in the absence of law, he has freedom of movement. What purpose, moreover, would a looting expedition effect in

a country, which throughout its extent is occupied only by grubbing peasants? The peasant can carry off from the peasant nothing
which he does not already own.   In a condition
of society marked by superfluity of agricultural land, each individual contributes only a
little work to its extensive cultivation. Each
occupies as much territory as he needs. More
would be superfluous. Its acquisition would
be lost labor, even were its owner able to con-
serve for any length of time the grain products
thus secured. Under primitive conditions,
however, this spoils rapidly by reason of change
of atmosphere, ants, or other agencies. According to Ratzel, the Central African peasant must convert the superfluous portion of his
crops into beer as quickly as possible in order
not to lose it entirely!

For all these reasons, primitive peasants are
totally lacking in that warlike desire to take the
offensive which is the distinguishing mark of
hunters and herdsmen: war can not better their
condition. And this peaceable attitude is
strengthened by the fact that the occupation of

the peasant does not make him an efficient warrior. It is true his muscles are strong and he has powers of endurance, but he is sluggish of movement and slow to come to a determination, while huntsmen and nomads by their methods of living develop speed of motion and swiftness of action. For this reason, the primitive peasant is usually of a more gentle disposition than they.*

To sum up: within the economic and social conditions of the peasant districts, one finds no differentiation working for the higher forms of integration. There exists neither the impulse nor the possibility for the warlike subjection of neighbors. No "State" can there-

* This psychological contradiction, though often expressly stated, is not the absolute rule, Grosse, *Forms of the Family*, says (page 137): "Some historians of civilization place the peasant in opposition to the warlike nomads, claiming that the peasants are peace-loving peoples. In fact one can not state that their economic life leads them to wars, or educates them for it, as can be said of stock raisers. Nevertheless, one finds within the scope of this form of cultivation a mass of the most warlike and cruel peoples to be found anywhere. The wild cannibals of the Bismarck archipelago, the blood-lusting Vitians, the butchers of men of Dahome and Ashanti —they all cultivate the 'peaceable' acres; and if other peasants are not quite as bad, it seems that the kindly disposition of the vast mass appears to be, at least, questionable."

fore arise; and, as a matter of fact, none ever
has arisen from such social conditions.   Had
there been no impulse from without, from
groups of men nourished in a different manner, the primitive grubber would never have
discovered the State.

(c) PEOPLES PRECEDING THE STATE:
HERDSMEN AND VIKINGS

Herdsmen, on the contrary, even though
isolated, have developed a whole series of the
elements of statehood; and in the tribes which
have progressed further, they have developed
this in its totality, with the single exception
of the last point of identification which completes the state in its modern sense, that is to
say, with exception only of the definitive occupation of a circumscribed territory.

One of these elements is an economic one.
Even without the intervention of extra-economic force, there may still develop among
herd men a sufficiently marked differentiation
of property and income.   Assuming that, at
the start, there was complete equality in the

number of cattle, yet within a short time, the one man may be richer and the other poorer. An especially clever breeder will see his herd increase rapidly, while an especially careful watchman and bold hunter will preserve his from decimation by beasts of prey. The element of luck also affects the result. One of these herders finds an especially good grazing ground and healthful watering places; the other one loses his entire stock through pestilence, or through a snowfall or a sandstorm.

Distinctions in fortune quickly bring about class distinctions. The herdsman who has lost all must hire himself to the rich man; and sinking thus under the other, become dependent on him. Wherever herdsmen live, from all three parts of the ancient world, we find the same story. Meitzen reports of the Lapps, nomadic in Norway: "Three hundred reindeer sufficed for one family; who owned only a hundred must enter the service of the richer, whose herds ran up to a thousand head." [6] The same writer, speaking of the Central Asiatic Nomads, says: "A family required three hundred head of cattle for comfort; one hundred head is poverty, followed by a life of debt. The servant must cultivate the lands of the lord." [7]   Ratzel reports concerning the Hottentots of Africa a form of "commendatio": "The poor man endeavors to hire himself to the rich man, his only object being to obtain cattle." [8]   Laveleye, who reports the same circumstances from Ireland, traces the origin and the name of the feudal system (*système féodal*) to the loaning of cattle by the rich to the poor members of the tribe; accordingly, a "fee-od" (owning of cattle) was the first feud whereby so long as the debt existed the magnate bound the small owner to himself as "his man."

We can only hint at the methods whereby, even in peaceable associations of herdsmen, this economic and consequent social differentiation may have been furthered by the connection of the patriarchate with the offices of supreme and sacrificial priesthood if the wise old men used cleverly the superstition of their clan associates. But this differentiation, so long as it is unaffected by the political means, operates within very modest bounds. Cleverness and efficiency are not hereditary with any degree of certainty. The largest herd will be split up if many heirs grow up in one tent, and fortune is tricky. In our own day, the richest man among the Lapps of Sweden, in the shortest possible time, has been reduced to such complete poverty that the government has had to support him. All these causes bring it about that the original condition of economic and social equality is always approximately restored. "The more peaceable, aboriginal, and genuine the nomad is, the smaller are the tangible differences of possession. It is touching to note the pleasure with which an old prince of the Tsaidam Mongols accepts his tribute or gift, consisting of a handful of tobacco, a piece of sugar, and twenty-five kopeks." [9]

This equality is destroyed permanently and in greater degree by the political means. "Where war is carried on and booty acquired, greater differences arise, which find their expression in the ownership of slaves, women, arms and spirited mounts." [10]

The ownership of *slaves!* The nomad is the inventor of slavery, and thereby has created the seedling of the state; the first economic exploitation of man by man.

The huntsman carries on wars and takes captives. But he does not make them slaves; either he kills them, or else he adopts them into the tribe. Slaves would be of no use to him. The booty of the chase can be stowed away even less than grain can be "capitalized." The idea of using a human being as a labor motor could only come about on an economic plane on which a body of wealth has developed, call it capital, which can be increased only with the assistance of dependent labor forces.

This stage is first reached by the herdsmen. The forces of one family, lacking outside assistance, suffice to hold together a herd of very limited size, and to protect it from attacks of beasts of prey or human enemies. Until the political means is brought into play, auxiliary forces are found very sparingly; such as the poorer members of the clan already mentioned, together with runaways from foreign tribes, who are found all over the world as protected dependents in the suite of the greater owners of herds.[11]   In some cases, an entire poor clan of herdsmen enters, half freely, into the service of some rich tribe.   "Entire peoples take positions corresponding to their relative wealth. Thus the Tungusen, who are very poor, try to live near the settlements of the Tschuktsches, because they find occupation as herdsmen of the reindeer belonging to the wealthy Tschuktsches; they are paid in reindeer.   And the subjection of the Ural-Samojedes by the Sirjaenes came about through the gradual occupation of their pasturing grounds." [12]

Excepting, however, the last named case, which is already very state-like, the few existing labor forces, without capital, are not sufficient to permit the clan to keep very large herds.   Furthermore, methods of herding themselves compel division.   For a pasture may not, as they say in the Swiss Alps, be "overpushed," that is to say, have too many

cattle on it. The danger of losing the entire
stock is reduced by the measure in which it is
distributed over various pastures. For cattle
plagues, storms, etc., can affect only a part;
while even the enemy from abroad can not drive
off all at once. For that reason, the Hereros,
for example, "find every well-to-do owner
forced to keep, besides the main herd, several
other subsidiary herds. Younger brothers or
other near relatives, or in want of these, tried
old servants, watch them." [13]

For that reason, the developed nomad spares
his captured enemy; he can use him as a slave
on his pasture. We may note this transition
from killing to enslaving in a customary rite
of the Scythians: they offered up at their
places of sacrifice one out of every hundred
captured enemies. Lippert, who reports this,
sees in it "the beginning of a limitation, and
the reason thereof is evidently to be found in
the value which a captured enemy has acquired
by becoming the servant of a tribal herdsman." [14]

With the introduction of slaves into the tribal economy of the herdsmen, the state, in its essential elements, is completed, except that it has not as yet acquired a definitely circumscribed territorial limit. The state has thus the *form* of dominion, and its economic basis is the exploitation of human labor. Henceforth, economic differentiation and the formation of social classes progress rapidly. The herds of the great, wisely divided and better guarded by numerous armed servants than those of the simple freemen, as a rule, maintain themselves at their original number: they also increase faster than those of the freemen, since they are augmented by the greater share in the booty which the rich receive, corresponding to the number of warriors (slaves) which these place in the field.

Likewise, the office of supreme priest creates an ever-widening cleft which divides the numbers of the clan, all formerly equals; until finally a genuine nobility, the rich descendants of the rich patriarchs, is placed in juxtaposition to the ordinary freemen. "The redskins have also in their progressive organization developed no nobility and no slavery,* and in this their organization distinguishes itself most essentially from those of the old world.   Both arise from the development of the patriarchate of stock-raising people." [15]

Thus we find, with all developed tribes of herdsmen, a social separation into three distinct classes: nobility ("head of the house of his fathers" in the biblical phrase), common freemen and slaves.   According to Mommsen, "all Indo-Germanic people have slavery as a jural institution." [16]   This applies to the Arians and the Semites of Asia and Africa as well as to the Hamites.   Among all the Fulbe of the Sahara, "society is divided into princes, chieftains, commons and slaves." [17]   And we find the same facts everywhere, as a matter of course, wherever slavery is legally established, as among the Hova [18] and their Polynesian kinsmen, the "Sea Nomads."   Human psychology under similar circumstances brings

* This statement of Lippert is not quite correct. The higher developed domiciled huntsmen and fishermen of Northwest America have both nobles and slaves. also Natchez.

about like conditions, independent of color or race.

Thus the herdsman gradually becomes accustomed to earning his livelihood through warfare, and to the exploitation of men as servile labor motors. And one must admit that his entire mode of life impels him to make more and more use of the "political means."

He is physically stronger and just as adroit and determined as the primitive huntsman, whose food supply is too irregular to permit him to.attain his greatest natural physical development. The herdsman can, in all cases, grow to his full stature, since he has uninterrupted nourishment in the milk of his herds and an unfailing supply of meat. This is shown in the Arian horse nomad, no less than in the herdsman of Asia and Africa, e. g., the Zulu. Secondly, tribes of herdsmen increase faster than hordes of hunters. This is so, not only because the adults can obtain much more nourishment from a given territory, but still more because possession of the milk of animals shortens the period of nursing for the mothers, and consequently permits a greater number of children to be born and to grow to maturity. As a consequence, the pastures and steppes of the old world became inexhaustible fountains, which periodically burst their confines letting loose inundations of humanity, so that they came to be called the *"vaginæ gentium."*   ! / !

Moreover we find a much larger number of armed warriors among herdsmen than among hunters. Each one of these herdsmen is stronger individually, and yet all of them together are at least as mobile as is a horde of huntsmen; while the camel and horse riders among them are incomparably more mobile. This greater mass of the best individual elements is held together by an organization only possible under the ægis of a slave-holding patriarchate accustomed to rule, an organization prepared and developed by its occupation, and therefore superior to that of the young warriors of the huntsmen sworn to the service of one chief.

Hunters, it may be observed, work best alone or in small groups. Herdsmen, on the other hand, move to the best advantage in a great train, in which each individual is best protected; and which is in every sense an armed expedition, where every stopping place becomes an armed camp. Thus there is developed a science of tactical maneuvers, strict subordination, and firm discipline. "One does not make a mistake," as Ratzel says, "if one accounts as the disciplinary forces in the life of the nomads the order of the tents which, in the same form, exists since most ancient times. Every one and everything here has a definite, traditional place; hence the speed and order in setting up and in breaking camp, in establishment and in rearrangement. It is unheard of that any one without orders, or without the most pressing reason, should change his place. Thanks to this strict discipline, the tents can be packed up and loaded away within the space of an hour." [19]

The same tried order, handed down from untold ages, regulates the warlike march of the tribe of herdsmen while on the hunt, in war and in peaceable wandering. Thus they become professional fighters, irresistible until the state develops higher and mightier organizations. Herdsman and warrior become identical concepts) Ratzel's statement concerning the Central Asiatic Nomads applies to them all: ("The nomad is, as herdsman, an economic, as warrior, a political concept) It is easy for him to turn from any activity to that of the warrior and robber. Everything in life has for him a pacific and war-like, an honest and robber-like, side; according to circumstances, the one or the other of these phases appears uppermost. Even fishing and navigation, at the hands of the East Caspian Turkomans, developed into piracy. . . . The activities of the apparently pacific existence as a herdsman determine those of the warrior; the pastoral crook becomes a fighting implement. In the fall, when the horses return strengthened from the pasture and the second cropping of the sheep is completed, the nomads' minds turn to some feud or robbing expedition (*Baranta*, literally, to make cattle, to lift cattle), adjourned to that time. This is an ex-

pression of the right of self help, which in con-
tentions over points of law, or in quarrels affecting dignity, or in blood feuds, seeks both
requital and surety in the most valuable things
that the enemy possesses, namely, the animals
of his herd. Young men who have not been
on a *baranta* must first acquire the name *batir*,
hero, and thus earn the claim to honor and respect. The pleasure of ownership joined to
the desire for adventure develops the triple
descending gradation of avenger, hero and
robber." [20]

An identical development takes place with
the sea nomads, the "Vikings," as with the land
nomads. This is quite natural, since in the
most important cases noted in the history of
mankind, sea nomads are simply land nomads
taking to the sea.

We have noted above one of the innumerable examples which indicate that the herdsman does not long hesitate to use for maraud-
ing expeditions, instead of the horse or the
"ship of the desert," the "horses of the sea."
This case is exemplified by the East Caspian

Turkomans.[21]   Another example is furnished by the Scythians: "From the moment when they learn from their neighbors the art of navigating the seas, these wandering herdsmen, whom Homer (*Iliad,* XIII, 8) calls 'respected horsemen, milk-eaters and poor, the most just of men,' change into daring navigators like their Baltic and Scandinavian brethren. Strabo (*Cas.,* 801) complains: 'Since they have ventured on the sea, carrying on piracy and murdering foreigners, they have become worse; and associating with many peoples, they adopt their petty trading and spendthrift habits.' " [22]

If the Phœnicians really were "Semites," they furnish an additional example of incomparable importance of the transformation of land into "sea Bedouins," i. e., warlike robbers; and the same is probably true for the majority of the numerous peoples who looted the rich countries around the Mediterranean, whether from the coast of Asia Minor, Dalmatia, or from the North African shore. These begin from the earliest times, as we see from the Egyptian monuments (the Greeks were not admitted into Egypt),[23] and continue to the present day: e. g., the Riff pirates. The North African "Moors," an amalgamation of Arabs and of Berbers, both originally land nomads, are perhaps the most celebrated example of this change.

There are cases in which sea nomads—that is to say, sea robbers—arise immediately from fishermen, with no intermediate herdsman stage. We have already examined the causes which give the herdsmen their superiority over the peasantry: the relatively numerous population of the horde, combined with an activity which develops courage and quick resolution in the individual, and educates the mass as a whole to tense discipline. All this applies also to fishermen dwelling on the sea. Rich fishing grounds permit a considerable density of population, as is shown in the case of the Northwest Indians (Tlinkit, etc.); these permit also the keeping of slaves, since the slave earns more by fishing than his keep amounts to.

Thus we find, here alone among the redskins, slavery developed as an institution; and we find, therefore, along with it, permanent economic differences among the freemen, which result in a sort of plutocracy similar to that noted among herdsmen. Here, as there, the habit of command over slaves produces the habit of rule and a taste for the "political means." This is favored by the tense discipline developed in navigation. "Not the least advantage of fishing in common is found in the discipline of the crews. They must render implicit obedience to a leader chosen in each of the larger fishing boats, since every success depends upon obedience. The command of a ship afterward facilitates the command of the state. We are accustomed to reckon the Solomon Islanders as complete savages, and yet their life is subject to one solitary element, which combines their forces, namely, navigation." [24] If the Northwest Indians did not become such celebrated sea robbers as their likes in the old world, this is due to the fact that the neighborhoods within their reach had developed no rich civilization; but all more developed fishermen carry on piracy.

For this reason, the Vikings have the same capacity to choose the political means as the basis of their economic existence as have the cattle raiders; and similarly they have been founders of states on a large scale. Hereafter, we shall distinguish the states founded by them as "sea states," while the states founded by herdsmen—and in the new world by hunters—will be called "land states." Sea states will be treated extensively when we discuss the consequences of the *developed feudal state*. As long, however, as we are discussing the development of the state, and the *primitive* feudal state, we must limit ourselves to the consideration of the land state and leave the sea state out of account. This treatment is convenient, since in all essential things the sea state has the same characteristics, but its development can not be followed through the various typical stages as can the development of the land state.

(d) THE GENESIS OF THE STATE

The hordes of huntsmen are incomparably
weaker, both in numbers and in the strength of
the single fighters, than are the herdsmen with
whom they occasionally brush. Naturally
they can not withstand the impact. They flee
to the highlands and mountains, where the
herdsmen have no inclination to follow them,
not only because of the physical hardships involved, but also because their cattle do not find
pasturage there; or else they enter into a form
of cliental relation, as happened often in
Africa, especially in very ancient times.
When the Hyksos invaded Egypt, such dependent huntsmen followed them. The huntsmen usually pay for protection an inconsider-
able tribute in the form of spoils of the chase,
and are used for reconnoitering and watching.
But the huntsman, being a "practical anar-
chist," often invites his own destruction rather
than submit to regular labor. For these reasons, no "state" ever arose from such contact.

The peasants fight as undisciplined levies,

and with their single combatants undisciplined;
so that, in the long run, even though they are
strong in numbers, they are no more able than
are the hunters to withstand the charge of
the heavily armed herdsmen. But the peasantry do not flee. The peasant is attached to
his ground, and has been used to regular work.
He remains, yields to subjection, and pays
tribute to his conqueror; *that is the genesis of
the land states in the old world.*

In the new world, where the larger herding
animals, cattle, horses, camels, were not indig-
enous, we find that instead of the herdsman
the hunter is the conqueror of the peasant,
because of his infinitely superior adroitness in
the use of arms and in military discipline. "In
the old world we found that the contrast of
herdsmen and peasants developed civilization;
in the new world the contrast is between the
sedentary and the roving tribes. The Tol-
tecks, devoted to agriculture, fought wild
tribes (with a highly developed military
organization) breaking in from the north, as
endlessly as did Iran with Turan." [25]

This applies not only to Peru and Mexico, but to all America, a strong ground for the opinion that the fundamental basis of civilization is the same all over the world, its development being consistent and regular under the most varied economic and geographical conditions. Wherever opportunity offers, and man possesses the power, he prefers political to economic means for the preservation of his life. And perhaps this is true not alone of man, for, according to Maeterlinck's *Life of the Bees,* a swarm which has once made the experiment of obtaining honey from a foreign hive, by robbery instead of by tedious building, is thenceforth spoiled for the "economic means." From working bees, robber bees have developed.

Leaving out of account the state formations of the new world, which have no great significance in universal history, the cause of the genesis of all states is the contrast between peasants and herdsmen, between laborers and robbers, between bottom lands and prairies. Ratzel, regarding sociology from the geo-

graphical view-point, expresses this cleverly:
"It must be remembered that nomads do not
always destroy the opposing civilization of the
settled folk. This applies not only to tribes,
but also to states, even to those of some might.
The war-like character of the nomads is a
great factor in the creation of states. It finds
expression in the immense nations of Asia controlled by nomad dynasties and nomad armies,
such as Persia, ruled by the Turks; China,
conquered and governed by the Mongols and
Manchus; and in the Mongol and Radjaputa
states of India, as well as in the states on
the border of the Soudan, where the. amalgamation of the formerly hostile elements has
not yet developed so far, although they are
joined together by mutual benefit. In no
place is it shown so clearly as here on the
border of the nomad and peasant peoples, that
the great workings of the impulse making for
civilization on the part of the nomads are not
the result of civilizing activity, but of war-like
exploits at first detrimental to pacific work.
Their importance lies in the capacity of the

nomads to hold together the sedentary races who otherwise would easily fall apart. This, however, does not exclude their learning much from their subjects. . . . Yet all these industrious and clever folk did not have and could not have the will and the power to rule, the military spirit, and the sense for the order and subordination that befits a state. For this reason, the desert-born lords of the Soudan rule over their negro folk just as the Manchus rule their Chinese subjects. This takes place pursuant to a law, valid from Timbuctoo to Pekin, whereby advantageous state formations arise in rich peasant lands adjoining a wide prairie; where a high material culture of sedentary peoples is violently subjugated to the service of prairie dwellers having energy, war-like capacity, and desire to rule." [26]

In the genesis of the state, from the subjection of a peasant folk by a tribe of herdsmen or by sea nomads, six stages may be distinguished. In the following discussion it should not be assumed that the actual historical development must, in each particular case, climb the entire scale step by step. Although, even here, the argument does not depend upon bare theoretical construction, since every particular stage is found in numerous examples, both in the world's history and in ethnology, and there are states which have apparently progressed through them all. But there are many more which have skipped one or more of these stages.

The first stage comprises robbery and killing in border fights, endless combats broken neither by peace nor by armistice. It is marked by killing of men, carrying away of children and women, looting of herds, and burning of dwellings. Even if the offenders are defeated at first, they return in stronger and stronger bodies, impelled by the duty of blood feud. Sometimes the peasant group may assemble, may organize its militia, and perhaps temporarily defeat the nimble enemy; but mobilization is too slow and supplies to be brought into the desert too costly for the peasants. The peasants' militia does not, as does the enemy, carry its stock of food—its herds— with it into the field. In Southwest Africa the

Germans recently experienced the difficulties which a well-disciplined and superior force, equipped with a supply train, with a railway reaching back to its base of supply, and with the millions of the German Empire behind it, may have with a handful of herdsmen warriors, who were able to give the Germans a decided setback. In the case of primitive levies, this difficulty is increased by the narrow spirit of the peasant, who considers only his own neighborhood, and by the fact that while the war is going on the lands are uncultivated. Therefore, in such cases, in the long run, the small but compact and easily mobilized body constantly defeats the greater disjointed mass, as the panther triumphs over the buffalo.

This is the first stage in the formation of states. The state may remain stationary at this point for centuries, for a thousand years. The following is a thoroughly characteristic example:

"Every range of a Turkoman tribe formerly bordered upon a wide belt which might be designated as its 'looting district.' Every-

thing north and east of Chorassan, though
nominally under Persian dominion, has for
decades belonged more to the Turkomans,
Jomudes, Goklenes, and other tribes of the
bordering plains, than to the Persians. The
Tekinzes, in a similar manner, looted all the
stretches from Kiwa to Bokhara, until other
Turkoman tribes were successfully rounded
up either by force or by corruption to act as
a buffer. Numberless further instances can
be found in the history of the chain of oases
which extends between Eastern and Western
Asia directly through the steppes of its central part, where since ancient times the
Chinese have exercised a predominant influence through their possession of all important
strategic centers, such as the Oasis of Chami.
The nomads, breaking through from north
and south, constantly tried to land on these
islands of fertile ground, which to them must
have appeared like Islands of the Blessed.
And every horde, whether laden down with
booty or fleeing after defeat, was protected by
the plains. Although the most immediate

threats were averted by the continued weakening of the Mongols, and the actual dominion of Thibet, yet the last insurrection of the Dunganes showed how easily the waves of a mobile tribe break over these islands of civilization. Only after the destruction of the nomads, impossible as long as there are open plains in Central Asia, can their existence be definitely secured." [27]

The entire history of the old world is replete with well-known instances of mass expeditions, which must be assigned to the first stage of state development, inasmuch as they were intent, not upon conquest, but directly on looting. Western Europe suffered through these expeditions at the hands of the Celts, Germans, Huns, Avars, Arabs, Magyars, Tartars, Mongolians and Turks by land; while the Vikings and the Saracens harassed it on the waterways. These hordes inundated entire continents far beyond the limits of their accustomed looting ground. They disappeared, returned, were absorbed, and left behind them only wasted lands. In many cases, however, they advanced

in some part of the inundated district directly
to the sixth and last stage of state formation,
in cases namely, where they established a permanent dominion over the peasant population.
Ratzel describes these mass migrations ex-
cellently in the following:

"The expeditions of the great hordes of
nomads contrast with this movement, drop by
drop and step by step, since they overflow
with tremendous power, especially Central
Asia and all neighboring countries. The
nomads of this district, as of Arabia and
Northern Africa, unite mobility in their way of
life with an organization holding together their
entire mass for one single object. It seems to
be a characteristic of the nomads that they
easily develop despotic power and far-reaching might from the patriarchal cohesion of the
tribe. Mass governments thereby come into
being, which compare with other movements
among men in the same way that swollen
streams compare with the steady but diffused
flow of a tributary. The history of China,
India, and Persia, no less than that of Europe,

shows their historical importance. Just as
they moved about on their ranges with their
wives and children, slaves and carts, herds and
all their paraphernalia, so they inundated the
borderlands. While this ballast may have deprived them of speed it increased their momentum. The frightened inhabitants were
driven before them, and like a wave they rolled
over the conquered countries, absorbing their
wealth. Since they carried everything with
them, their new abodes were equipped with all
their possessions, and thus their final settlements were of an ethnographic importance.
After this manner, the Magyars flooded Hungary, the Manchus invaded China, the Turks,
the countries from Persia to the Adriatic." [28]

What has been said here of Hamites, Semites and Mongolians, may be said also, at least
in part, of the Arian tribes of herdsmen. It
applies also to the true negroes, at least to
those who live entirely from their herds:
"The mobile, warlike tribes of the Kafirs possess a power of expansion which needs only
an enticing object in order to attain violent

effects and to overturn the ethnologic relations of vast districts. Eastern Africa offers such an object. Here the climate did not forbid stock raising, as in the countries of the interior, and did not paralyze from the start, the power of impact of the nomads, while nevertheless numerous peaceable agricultural peoples found room for their development. Wandering tribes of Kafirs poured like devastating streams into the fruitful lands of the Zambesi, and up to the highlands between the Tanganyika and the coast. Here they met the advance guard of the Watusi, a wave of Hamite eruption, coming from the north. The former inhabitants of these districts were either exterminated, or as serfs cultivated the lands which they formerly owned; or they still continued to fight; or again, they remained undisturbed in settlements left on one side by the stream of conquest." [29]

All this has taken place before our eyes. Some of it is still going on. During many thousands of years it has "jarred all Eastern Africa from the Zambesi to the Mediterranean." The incursion of the Hyksos, whereby for over five hundred years Egypt was subject to the shepherd tribes of the eastern and northern deserts—"kinsmen of the peoples who up to the present day herd their stock between the Nile and the Red Sea" [30]— is the first authenticated foundation of a state. These states were followed by many others both in the country of the Nile itself, and farther southward, as far as the Empire of Muata Jamvo on the southern rim of the central Congo district, which Portuguese traders in Angola reported as early as the end of the sixteenth century, and down to the Empire of Uganda, which only in our own day has finally succumbed to the superior military organization of Europe. "Desert land and civilization never lie peaceably alongside one another; but their battles are all alike and full of repetitions." [31]

"Alike and full of repetitions"! That may be said of universal history on its basic lines. The human ego in its fundamental aspect is much the same all the world over. It acts uniformly, in obedience to the same influences of its environment, with races of all colors, in all parts of the earth, in the tropics as in the temperate zones. One must step back far enough and choose a point of view so high that the variegated aspect of the details does not hide the great movements of the mass. In such a case, our eye misses the "mode" of fighting, wandering, laboring humanity, while its "substance," ever similar, ever new, ever enduring through change, reveals itself under uniform laws.

Gradually, from this first stage, there develops the second, in which the peasant, through thousands of unsuccessful attempts at revolt, has accepted his fate and has ceased every resistance. About this time, it begins to dawn on the consciousness of the wild herdsman that a murdered peasant can no longer plow, and that a fruit tree hacked down will no longer bear. In his own interest, then, wherever it is possible, he lets the peasant live and the tree stand. The expedition of the herdsmen comes just as before, every member bristling with arms, but no longer intending nor expecting war and violent appropriation. The raiders burn and kill only so far as is necessary to enforce a wholesome respect, or to break an isolated resistance. But in general, principally in accordance with a developing customary right—the first germ of the development of all public law—the herdsman now appropriates only the surplus of the peasant. That is to say, he leaves the peasant his house, his gear and his provisions up to the next crop.* The herdsman in the first stage is like the bear, who for the purpose of robbing the beehive, destroys it. In the second stage he is like the bee-keeper, who leaves the bees enough honey to carry them through the winter.

Great is the progress between the first stage and the second. Long is the forward step,

* Ratzel, l. c. II, page 393, in speaking of the Arabs says: "The difficulty of nourishing slaves makes it impossible to keep them. Vast populations are kept in subjection and deprived of everything beyond the necessaries for maintaining life. They turn entire oases into demesne lands, visited at the harvest time in order to rob the inhabitants; a domination characteristic of the desert."

both economically and politically. In the beginning, as we have seen, the acquisition by
the tribe of herdsmen was purely an occupying one. Regardless of consequences, they destroyed the source of future wealth for the enjoyment of the moment. Henceforth the acquisition becomes economical, because all
economy is based on wise housekeeping, or in
other words, on restraining the enjoyment of
the moment in view of the needs of the future.
The herdsman has learned to "capitalize." It
is a vast step forward in politics when an utterly strange human being, prey heretofore
like the wild animals, obtains a value and is
recognized as a source of wealth. Although
this is the beginning of all slavery, subjugation, and exploitation, it is at the same time
the genesis of a higher form of society, that
reaches out beyond the family based upon
blood relationship. We saw how, between the
robbers and the robbed, the first threads of a
jural relation were spun across the cleft which
separated those who had heretofore been only
"mortal enemies." The peasant thus obtains

a semblance of *right* to the bare necessaries of life; so that it comes to be regarded as *wrong* to kill an unresisting man or to strip him of everything.

And better than this, gradually more delicate and softer threads are woven into a net very thin as yet, but which, nevertheless, brings about more human relations than the customary arrangement of the division of spoils. Since the herdsmen no longer meet the peasants in combat only, they are likely now to grant a respectful request, or to remedy a well grounded grievance. "The categorical imperative" of equity, "Do to others as you would have them do unto you," had heretofore ruled the herdsmen only in their dealings with their own tribesmen and kind. Now for the first time it begins to speak, shyly whispering in behalf of those who are alien to blood relationship. In this, we find the germ of that magnificent process of external amalgamation which, out of small hordes, has formed nations and unions of nations; and which, in the future is to give life to the concept of "humanity."

We find also the germ of the internal unifica-
tion of tribes once separated, from which, in
place of the hatred of "barbarians," will come
the all comprising love of humanity, of Christianity and Buddhism.

*The moment when first the conqueror
spared his victim in order permanently to exploit him in productive work, was of incomparable historical importance. It gave birth
to nation and state, to right and the higher
economics, with all the developments and rami-
fications which have grown and which will
hereafter grow out of them.* The root of
everything human reaches down into the dark
soil of the animal—love and art, no less than
state, justice and economics.

Still another tendency knots yet more closely
these psychic relations. To return to the comparison of the herdsman and the bear, there are
in the desert, beside the bear who guards the
bees, other bears who also lust after honey.
But our tribe of herdsmen blocks their way,
and protects its beehives by force of arms.
The peasants become accustomed, when dan-

ger threatens, to call on the herdsmen, whom
they no longer regard as robbers and murder-
ers, but as protectors and saviors. Imagine
the joy of the peasants when the returning
band of avengers brings back to the village the
looted women and children, with the enemies'
heads or scalps. These ties are no longer,
threads, but strong and knotted bands.

Here is one of the principal forces of that
"integration," whereby in the further development, those originally not of the same blood,
and often enough of different groups speaking different languages, will in the end be
welded together into *one* people, with *one*
speech, *one* custom, and *one* feeling of nationality. This unity grows by degrees from common suffering and need, common victory
and defeat, common rejoicing and common
sorrow. A new and vast domain is open when
master and slave serve the same interests; then
arises a stream of sympathy, a sense of common service. Both sides apprehend, and
gradually recognize, each other's common humanity. Gradually the points of similarity

are sensed, in place of the differences in build and apparel, of language and religion, which had heretofore brought about only antipathy and hatred. Gradually they learn to understand one another, first through a common speech, and then through a common mental habit. The net of the psychical inter-relations becomes stronger.

In this second stage of the formation of states, the ground work, in its essentials, has been mapped out. No further step can be compared in importance to the transition whereby the bear becomes a bee-keeper. For this reason, short references must suffice.

The third stage arrives when the "surplus" obtained by the peasantry is brought by them regularly to the tents of the herdsmen as "tribute," a regulation which affords to both parties self-evident and considerable advantages. By this means, the peasantry is relieved entirely from the little irregularities connected with the former method of taxation, such as a few men knocked on the head, women violated, or farmhouses burned down. The herdsmen on the other hand, need no longer apply to this "business" any "expense" and labor, to use a mercantile expression; and they devote the time and energy thus set free toward an "extension of the works," in other words, to subjugating other peasants.

This form of tribute is found in many well-known instances in history: Huns, Magyars, Tartars, Turks, have derived their largest income from their European tributes. Sometimes the character of the tribute paid by the subjects to their master is more or less blurred, and the act assumes the guise of payment for protection, or indeed, of a subvention. The tale is well known whereby Attila was pictured by the weakling emperor at Constantinople as a vassal prince; while the tribute he paid to the Hun appeared as a fee.

The fourth stage, once more, is of very great importance, since it adds the decisive factor in the development of the state, as we are accustomed to see it, namely, the union on one strip of land of both ethnic groups.*   (It is well

* There is apparently in the case of the Fulbe, a transition

known that no jural definition of a state can be arrived at without the concept of state territory.) From now on, the relation of the two groups, which was originally international, gradually becomes more and more intranational,

This territorial union may be caused by foreign influences. It may be that stronger hordes have crowded the herdsmen forward, or that their increase in population has reached the limit set by the nutritive capacity of the steppes or prairies; it may be that a great cattle plague has forced the herdsmen to ex-

stage between the first three stages and the fourth, in which dominion is exercised half internationally and half intranationally. According to Ratzel (l. c. II, page 419): "Like a cuttle-fish, the conquering race stretches numerous arms hither and thither among the terrified aborigines, whose lack of cohesion affords plenty of gaps. Thus the Fulbe are slowly flowing into the Benue countries and quite gradually permeating them. Later observers have thus quite rightly abstained from assigning definite boundaries. There are many scattered Fulbe localities which look to a particular place as their center and as the center of their power. Thus Muri is the capital of the numerous Fulbe settlements scattered about the Middle Benue, and the position of Gola is similar in the Adamawa district. As yet there are no proper kingdoms with defined frontiers against each other and against independent tribes. Even these capitals are in other respects still far from being firmly settled."

change the unlimited scope of the prairies for
the narrows of some river valley. In general,
however, internal causes alone suffice to bring
it about that the herdsmen stay in the neighborhood of their peasants. The duty of protecting their tributaries against other "bears"
forces them to keep a levy of young warriors in
the neighborhood of their subjects; and this
is at the same time an excellent measure of defense since it prevents the peasants from giving way to a desire to break their bonds, or to
let some other herdsmen become their over-
lords. This latter occurrence is by no means
rare, since, if tradition is correct, it is the means
whereby the sons of Rurik came to Russia.

As yet the local juxtaposition does not mean
a state community in its narrowest sense; that
is to say, a unital organization.

In case the herdsmen are dealing with utterly unwarlike subjects, they carry on their
nomad life, peaceably wandering up and down
and herding their cattle among their perioike
and helots. This is the case with the light-
colored Wahuma,[32] "the handsomest men of

the world" (Kandt), in Central Africa, or the
Tuareg clan of the Hadanara of the Asgars,
"who have taken up their seats among the Imrad and have become wandering freebooters.
These Imrad are the serving class of the Asgars, who live on them, although the Imrad
could put into the field ten times as many warriors; the situation is analogous to that of the
Spartans in relation to their Helots." [33]   The
same may be said of the Teda among the
neighboring Borku: "Just as the land is divided into a semi-desert supporting the nomads, and gardens with date groves, so the
population is divided between nomads and settled folk.   Although about equal in number,
ten to twelve thousand altogether, it goes without saying that these latter are subject to the
others." [34]

And the same applies to the entire group of
herdsmen known as the Galla Masi and Wahuma. "Although differences in possessions
are considerable, they have few slaves, as a
serving class. These are represented by
peoples of a lower caste, who live separate and

apart from them. It is herdsmanship which is
the basis of the family, of the state, and along
with these of the principle of political evolution. In this wide territory, between Scehoa
and its southernmost boundaries, on the one
hand, and Zanzibar on the other, there is found
no strong political power, in spite of the highly
developed social articulation." [35]

In case the country is not adapted to herding cattle on a large scale—as was universally
the case in Western Europe—or where a less
unwarlike population might make attempts at
insurrection, the crowd of lords becomes more
or less permanently settled, taking either steep
places or strategically important points for
their camps, castles, or towns. From these
centers, they control their "subjects," mainly
for the purpose of gathering their tribute, paying no attention to them in other respects.
They let them administer their affairs, carry
on their religious worship, settle their disputes,
and adjust their methods of internal economy.
Their autochthonous constitution, their local
officials, are, in fact, not interfered with.

If Frants Buhl reports correctly, that was the beginning of the rule of the Israelites in Canaan.[36] Abyssinia, that great military force, though at the first glance it may appear to be a fully developed state, does not, however, seem to have advanced beyond the fourth stage. At least Ratzel states: "The principal care of the Abyssinians consists in the tribute, in which they follow the method of oriental monarchs in olden and modern times, which is not to interfere with the internal management and administration of justice of their subject peoples."[37]

The best example of the fourth stage is found in the situation in ancient Mexico before the Spanish conquest: "The confederation under the leadership of the Mexicans had somewhat more progressive ideas of conquest. Only those tribes were wiped out that offered resistance. In other cases, the vanquished were merely plundered, and then required to pay tribute. The defeated tribe governed itself just as before, through its own officials. It was different in Peru, where the formation

of a compact empire followed the first attack.
In Mexico, intimidation and exploitation were
the only aims of the conquest.   And so it came
about that the so-called Empire of Mexico at
the time of the conquest represented merely a
group of intimidated Indian tribes, whose federation with one another was prevented by
their fear of plundering expeditions from some
unassailable fort in their midst." [38]   It will be
observed that one can not speak of this as a
state in any proper sense.   Ratzel shows this
in the note following the above: "It is certain
that the various points held in subjection by
the warriors of Montezuma were separated
from one another by stretches of territory not
yet conquered.   A condition very like the rule
of the Hova in Madagascar.   One would not
say that scattering a few garrisons, or better
still, military colonies, over the land, is a mark
of absolute dominion, since these colonies, with
great trouble, maintain a strip of a few miles
in subjection." [39]

The logic of events presses quickly from the
fourth to the fifth stage, and fashions almost

completely the full state. Quarrels arise between neighboring villages or clans, which the lords no longer permit to be fought out, since by this the capacity of the peasants for service would be impaired. The lords assume the right to arbitrate, and in case of need, to enforce their judgment. In the end, it happens that at each "court" of the village king or chief of the clan there is an official deputy who exercises the power, while the chiefs are permitted to retain the appearance of authority. The state of the Incas shows, in a primitive condition, a typical example of this arrangement.

Here we find the Incas united at Cuzco where they had their patrimonial lands and dwellings.[40] A representative of the Incas, the Tucricuc, however, resided in every district at the court of the native chieftain. He " had supervision over all affairs of his district; he raised the troops, superintended the delivery of the tribute, ordered the forced labor on roads and bridges, superintended the administration of justice, and in short supervised everything in his district." [41]

The same institutions which have been developed by American huntsmen and Semite shepherds are found also among African herdsmen. In Ashanti, the system of the Tucricuc has been developed in a typical fashion; [42] and the Dualla have established for their subjects living in segregated villages "an institution based on conquest midway between a feudal system and slavery." [43] The same author reports that the Barotse have a constitution corresponding to the earliest stage of the mediæval feudal organization: "Their villages are . . . as a rule surrounded by a circle of hamlets where their serfs live. These, till the fields of their lords in the immediate neighborhood, grow grain, or herd the cattle." [44] The only thing that is not typical here consists in this, that the lords do not live in isolated castles or halls, but are settled in villages among their subjects.

It is only a very small step from the Incas to

the Dorians in Lacedæmon, Messenia, or
Crete; and no greater distance separates the
Fulbe, Dualla and Barotse from the comparatively rigidly organized feudal states of the
African Negro Empires of Uganda, Unyoro,
etc.; and the corresponding feudal empires of
Eastern and Western Europe and of all Asia.
In all places, the same results are brought
about by force of the same socio-psychological
causes. \ The necessity of keeping the subjects
in order and at the same time of maintaining
them at their full capacity for labor, leads step
by step from the fifth to the sixth stage, in
which the state, by acquiring full intra-nationality and by the evolution of "Nationality," is
developed in every sense. The need becomes
more and more frequent to interfere, to allay
difficulties, to punish, or to coerce obedience;
and thus develop the habit of rule and the
usages of government. The two groups, separated, to begin with, and then united on one
territory, are at first merely laid alongside one
another, then are scattered through one another like a mechanical mixture, as the term is

used in chemistry, until gradually they become more and more of a "chemical combination." They intermingle, unite, amalgamate to unity, in customs and habits, in speech and worship. Soon the bonds of relationship unite the upper and the lower strata. In nearly all cases the master class picks the handsomest virgins from the subject races for its concubines. A race of bastards thus develops, sometimes taken into the ruling class, sometimes rejected, and then because of the blood of the masters in their veins, becoming the born leaders of the subject race. In form and in content the primitive state is completed.

CHAPTER III

THE PRIMITIVE FEUDAL STATE

(a) THE FORM OF DOMINION

ITS form is domination; the dominion of a small warlike minority, interrelated and closely allied, over a definitely bounded territory and its cultivators. Gradually, custom develops some form of law in accordance with which this dominion is exercised. This law regulates the rights of primacy and the claims of the lords, and the duty of obedience and of service on the part of the subjects, in such wise that the capacity of the peasants for rendering service is not impaired. This word, *praestationsfaehigkeit,* dates from the reforms of Frederick the Great. The "bee-keepership," therefore, is governed by the law of custom. The duty of paying and working on the part of the peasants corresponds to the duty of protection on the part of the lords, who ward off exactions of their own companions, as well as defend the peasants from the attacks of foreign enemies.

Although this is one part of the content of the state concept, there is another, which in the beginning is of much greater magnitude; (the idea of economic exploitation, the political means for the satisfaction of needs.) The peasant surrenders a portion of the product of his labor, without any equivalent service in return. *"In the beginning was the ground rent."*

The forms under which the ground rent is collected or consumed vary. In some cases, the lords, as a closed union or community, are settled in some fortified camp and consume as communists the tribute of their peasantry. This is the situation in the state of the Inca. In some cases, each individual warrior-noble has a definite strip of land assigned to him: but generally the produce of this is still, as in Sparta, consumed in the "syssitia," by class associates and companions in arms. In some cases, the landed nobility scatters over the entire territory, each man housed with his following in his fortified castle, and consuming, each for himself; the produce of his dominion or lands. As yet these nobles have not become landlords, in the sense that they administer their property. Each of them receives tribute from the labor of his dependents, whom he neither guides nor supervises. This is the type of the mediæval dominion in the lands of the Germanic nobility. Finally, the knight becomes the owner and administrator of the knight's fee.* His former serfs develop into the laborers on his plantation, and the tribute now appears as the profit of the entrepreneur. This is the type of the earliest capitalist enterprise of modern times, the exploitation of large territories in the lands east of the Elbe, formerly occupied by Slavs and

* *Rittergutsbesitz* is the ultimate molecule of the German feudal system, a non-urban territory, approximating the concept of knight's fee in the Angevin fiscal legislation; in modern Germanic law, the possession of an acreage, alienable only as an entity, and by recent legislation, alienable to non-nobles, but subject to and capable of certain exceptions in law not inhering in other forms of real estate.—*Translator.*

later colonized by Germans. Numerous transitions lead from one stage to the other.

But always, in its essence, is the "State" the
same. Its purpose, in every case, is found to
be the political means for the satisfaction of
needs. (At first, its method is by exacting a
ground rent, so long as there exists no trade
activity the products of which can be appropriated. Its form, in every case, is that of
dominion, whereby exploitation is regarded as
"justice," maintained as a "constitution," insisted on strictly, and in case of need en-
forced with cruelty. And yet, in these ways,
the absolute right of the conqueror becomes
narrowed within the confines of law, for
the sake of permitting the continuous acquisition of ground rents. The duty of furnishing
supplies on the part of the subjects is limited
by their right to maintain themselves in good
condition. The right of taxation on the part
of the lords is supplemented by their duty to
afford protection within and without the state
—security under the law and defense of the
frontier.

At this point, the primitive state is completely developed in all its essentials. It has passed the embryonic condition; whatever follows can be only phenomena of growth.

As compared with unions of families, the state represents, doubtless, a much higher species; since the state embraces a greater mass of men, in closer articulation, more capable of conquering nature and of warding off enemies. It changes the half playful occupations of men into strict methodic labor, and thus brings untold misery to innumerable generations yet unborn. Henceforth, these must eat their bread in the sweat of their brow, since the golden age of the free community of blood relations has been followed by the iron rule of state dominion. But the state, by discovering labor in its proper sense, starts in this world that force which alone can bring about the golden age on a much higher plane of ethical relation and of happiness for all. The state, to use Schiller's words, destroys the untutored happiness of the people while they were children, in order to bring them along a sad path of suffering to the conscious happiness of maturity.

A higher species! Paul von Lilienfeld, one of the principal advocates of the view that society is an organism of a higher kind, has pointed out that in this respect an especially striking parallel can be drawn between ordinary organisms and this super-organism. All higher beings propagate sexually; lower beings asexually, by partition, by budding and sometimes by conjugation. We have shown that simple partition corresponds exactly to the growth and the further development of the association based on blood relationship, which existed before the state. This grows until it becomes too large for cohesion; it then loses its unity, divides, and the separate hordes, if they associate at all, remain in a very loose connection, without any sort of closer articulation. The amalgamation of exogamic groups is comparable to conjugation.

The state, however, comes into being through sexual propagation. All bisexual propagation is accomplished by the following

process: The male element, a small, very act-
ive, mobile, vibrating cell—the spermatozoön
—searches out a large inactive cell without
mobility of its own—the ovum, or female principle—enters and fuses with it.   From this
process, there results an immense growth; that
is to say, a wonderful differentiation with
simultaneous integration.   The inactive peasantry, bound by nature to their fields, is the
ovum, the mobile tribe of herdsmen the spermatozoön, of this sociologic act of fecundation;
and its resultant is the ripening of a higher social organism more fully differentiated in its
organs, and much more complete in its integra-
tions.   It is easy to find further parallels.
One may compare the border feuds to the
manner in which innumerable spermatozoa
swarm about the ovum until finally one, the
strongest or most fortunate, discovers and con-
quers the micropyle.   One may compare the
almost magical attraction which the ovum has
for the spermatozoön, to the no less magical
power by which the herdsmen from the steppes
are drawn into the cultivated plains.

But all this is no proof for the "organism."
The problem, however, has been pointed out.

(b) THE INTEGRATION

We have followed the genesis of the state,
from its second stage onward, in its objective
growth as a political and jural form with economic content. But it is far more important
to examine its subjective growth, its socio-
psychological "differentiation and integration," since all sociology is nearly always social
psychology. First, then, let us discuss integration.

We saw in the second stage, as set forth
above, how the net of psychical relations becomes ever tighter and closer enmeshed, as the
economic amalgamation advances. The two
dialects become one language; or one of the
two, often of an entirely different stock from
the other, becomes extinct. This, in some
cases, is the language of the victors, but
more frequently that of the vanquished.
Both cults amalgamate to one religion, in
which the tribal god of the conquerors is

adored as the principal divinity, while the old gods of the vanquished become either his servants, or, as demons or devils, his adversaries. The bodily type tends to assimilate, through the influence of the same climate and similar mode of living. Where a strong difference between the types existed or is maintained,[45] the bastards, to a certain extent, fill the gap—so that, in spite of the still existing ethnic contrast, everybody, more and more, begins to feel that the type of the enemies beyond the border is more strange, more "foreign" than is the new co-national type. Lords and subjects view one another as "we," at least as concerns the enemy beyond the border; and at length the memory of the different origin completely disappears. The conquerors are held to be the sons of the old gods. This, in many cases, they literally are, since these gods are nothing but the souls of their ancestors raised to godhead by apotheosis.

Since the new "states" are much more aggressive than the former communities bound together by mere blood relationship, the feeling of being different from the foreigner beyond the borders, growing in frequent feuds and wars, becomes stronger and stronger among those within the "realm of peace." And in the same measure there grows among them the feeling of belonging to another; so that the spirit of fraternity and of equity, which formerly existed only within the horde and which never ceased to hold sway within the association of nobles, takes root everywhere, and more and more finds its place in the relations between the lords and their subjects.

At first these relations are manifested only in infrequent cases: equity and fraternity are allowed only such play as is consistent with the right to use the political means; but that much is granted. A far stronger bond of psychical community between high and low, more potent than any success against foreign invasion, is woven by legal protection against the aggression of the mighty. *"Justitia fundamentum regnorum."* When, pursuant to their own ideals of justice, the aristocrats as a social group execute one of their own class for

murder or robbery, for having exceeded the
bounds of permitted exploitation, the thanks
and the joy of the subjects are even more heart-
felt than after victory over alien foes.

These, then, are the principal lines of development of the psychical integration. Common interest in maintaining order and law and
peace produce a strong feeling of solidarity,
which may be called "a consciousness of belonging to the same state."

(c) THE DIFFERENTIATION: GROUP THEORIES AND GROUP PSYCHOLOGY

On the other hand, as in all organic growth,
there develops *pari passu* a psychic differentiation just as powerful. The interests of the
group produce strong group feelings; the
upper and lower strata develop a "class consciousness" corresponding to their peculiar interests.

The separate interest of the master group
is served by maintaining intact the imposed
law of political means; such interest makes for
"conservatism." The interest of the subject

group, on the contrary, points to the removal
of the prevailing rule, to the substitution for
it of a new rule, the law of equality for all inhabitants of the state, and makes for "liberalism" and revolution.

Herein lies the tap root of all class and
party psychology. Hence there develop, in
accordance with definite psychological laws,
those incomparably mighty forms of thought
which, as "class theories," through thousands of
years of struggle guide and justify every social contest in the consciousness of contemporaries.

"When the will speaks reason has to be
silent," says Schopenhauer, or as Ludwig
Gumplowicz states the same idea, "Man acts
in accordance with laws of nature, as an after-
thought he thinks humanly." Man's will
being strictly "determined," he must act according to the pressure which the surrounding
world exerts upon him; and the same law is
valid for every community of men: groups,
classes, and the state itself. They "flow from
the plane of higher economic and social pres-

sure to that of lower pressure, along the line of least resistance." But every individual and each community of men believe themselves free agents; and therefore, by an unescapable psychical law they are forced to consider the path they are traversing as a freely chosen means, and the point toward which they are driven as a freely chosen end. And since man is a rational and ethical being, that is, a social entity, he is obliged to justify before reason and morality the method and the objective point of his movement, and to take account of the social consciousness of his time.

So long as the relations of both groups were simply those of internationally opposed border enemies, the exercise of the political means called for no justification, because a man of alien blood had no rights. As soon, however, as the psychic integration develops, in any degree, the community feeling of state consciousness, as soon as the bond servant acquires "rights," and the consciousness of essential equality percolates through the mass, the political means requires a system of justification;

and there arises in the ruling class the group theory of "legitimacy."

Everywhere, the upholders of legitimacy justify dominion and exploitation with similar anthropological and theological reasoning. The master group, since it recognizes bravery and warlike efficiency as the only virtues of a man, declares itself, the victors,—and from its standpoint quite correctly—to be the more efficient, the better "race." This point of view is the more intensified, the lower the subject race is reduced by hard labor and low fare. And since the tribal god of the ruling group has become the supreme god in the new amalgamated state religion, this religion declares— and again from its view-point quite correctly— that the constitution of the state has been decreed by heaven, that it is "tabu," and that interference with it is sacrilege. In consequence, therefore, of a simple logical inversion, the exploited or subject group is regarded as an essentially inferior race, as unruly, tricky, lazy, cowardly and utterly incapable of self-rule or self-defense, so that any up-

rising against the imposed dominion must nec-
essarily appear as a revolt against God Himself and against His moral ordinances. For
these reasons, the dominant group at all times
stands in closest union with the priesthood,
which, in its highest positions, at least, nearly
always recruits itself from their sons, sharing
their political rights and economic privileges.

This has been, and is at this day, the class
theory of the ruling group; nothing has been
taken from it, not an item has been added to it.
Even the very modern argument by which, for
example, the landed nobility of old France and
of modern Prussia attempted to put out of
court the claims of the peasantry to the ownership of lands, on the allegation that they had
owned the land from time immemorial, while
their peasants had only been granted a life
tenure therein,—is reproduced among the Wahuma, of Africa,[46] and probably could be
shown in many other instances.

Like their class theory, their class psychology has been, and is, at all times the same.
Its most important characteristic, the "aristo-

crat's pride," shows itself in contempt for the
lower laboring strata.) This is so inherent,
that herdsmen, even after they have lost their
herds and become economically dependent, still
retain their pride as former lords: "Even the
Galla, who have been despoiled of their wealth
of herds by the Somali north of the Tana, and
who thus have become watchers of other men's
herds, and even in some cases along the Sabaki
become peasants, still look with contempt upon
the peasant Watokomo, who are subject to
them and resemble the Suaheli. But their attitude is quite different toward their tributary
hunting peoples, namely, the Waboni, the
Wassanai, and the Walangulo (Ariangulo)
who resemble the Galla." [47]

The following description of the Tibbu
applies, as though it had been originally told
of them, to Walter Havenaught and the rest of
the poor knights who, in the crusades, looked
for booty and lordly domain. It applies no
less to many a noble fighting cock from Germany east of the Elbe, and to many a ragged
Polish gentleman. "They are men full of self-

consciousness. They may be beggars, but they are no pariahs. Many a people under these circumstances would be thoroughly miserable and depressed; the Tibbu have steel in their nature. They are splendidly fitted to be robbers, warriors, and rulers. Even their system of robbery is imposing, although it is base as a jackal's. These ragged Tibbus, fighting against extreme poverty and constantly on the verge of starvation, raise the most impudent claims with apparent or real belief in their validity. The right of the jackal, which regards the possessions of a stranger as common property, is the protection of greedy men against want. The insecurity of an all but perpetual state of war brings it about that life becomes an insistent challenge, and at the same time the reward of extortion!" [48]   This phenomenon is in nowise limited to Eastern Africa, for it is said of the Abyssinian soldier: "Thus equipped he comes along. Proudly he looks down on every one: his is the land, and for him the peasant must work." [49]

Deeply as the aristocrat at all times despises the economic means and the peasants who em-ploy it, he admits frankly his reliance on the political means. Honest war and "honest thievery" * are his occupation as a lord, are his good right.   His right—except over those who belong to the same clique—extends just as far as his power.   One finds this high praise of the political means nowhere so well stated as in the well-known Doric drinking song:

"I have great treasures; the spear and the sword;
  Wherewith to guard my body, the bull hide shield
    well tried.
With these I can plough, and harvest my crop,
  With these I can garner the sweet grape wine,
By them I bear the name 'Lord' with my serfs.

"But these never dare to bear spear and sword,
  Still less the guard of the body, the bull hide shield
    well tried.
They lie at my feet stretched out on the ground,
  My hand is licked by them as by hounds,
I am their Persian king—terrifying them by my
    name." [50]

In these wanton lines is expressed the pride

* Compare this with the prevalent justification of "honest graft" in municipal or political contracts.—*Translator*.

of warlike lords.   The following verses, taken
from an entirely different phase of civilization,
show that the robber still has part in the warrior in spite of Christianity, the Peace of God,
and the Holy Roman Empire of the German
Nation.   These lines also praise the political
means, but in its most crude form, simple robbery:

"Would you eke out your life, my young noble squire,
    Follow then my teaching, upon your horse and join
        the gang!
Take to the greenwood, when the peasant comes up,
    Run him down quickly, grab him then by the collar,
Rejoice in your heart, taking from him whatever he has,
    Unharness his horses and get you away!" [51]

"Unless," as Sombart adds, "he preferred
to hunt nobler game and to relieve merchants
of their valuable consignments.   The nobles
carried on robbery as a natural method of sup-
plementing their earnings, extending it more
and more as the income from their property no
longer sufficed to pay for the increasing demands of daily consumption and luxury.   The
system of freebooting was considered a
thoroughly honorable occupation, since it met

the demand of the essence of chivalry, that
every one should appropriate whatever was
within reach of his spear point or of the blade
of his sword. The nobles learned freebooting
as the cobbler was brought up to his trade.
The ballad has put this in merry wise:

> "To pillage, to rob, that is no shame,
> The best in the land do quite the same."

Besides this principal point of the "squire-
archical" psychology, a second distinguishing
mark scarcely less characteristic is found in the
piety of these folk whether it be of conviction
or merely, strongly accentuated in public.

It seems as though the same social ideas
always force identical characteristics on the ruling class. This is illustrated by the form under which God, in their view, appears as their
special National God and preponderatingly as
a God of War. Although they profess God
as the creator of all men, even of their enemies,
and since Christianity, as the God of Love, this
does not counteract the force with which class
interests formulate their appropriate ideol-
ogy.

In order to complete the sketch of the psychology of the ruling class, we must not forget the tendency to squander, easily understood in those "ignorant of the taste of toil," which appears sometimes in a higher form as generosity; nor must we forget, as their supreme trait, that death-despising bravery, which is called forth by the coercion imposed on a minority, their need to defend their rights at any time with arms, and which is favored by a freedom from all labor which permits the development of the body in hunting, sport and feuds. Its caricature is combativeness, and a supersensitiveness to personal honor, which degenerates into madness.

At this point a small digression: Cæsar found the Celts just at that stage of their development, in which the nobles had obtained dominion over their fellow clansmen. Since that time, his classic narrative has stood as a norm—their class psychology appears as the race psychology of all Celts. Not even Mommsen escaped this error. The result is that now, in every book on universal history or

sociology, one may read the palpable error, repeated until contradiction is of no avail, although a mere glance would have sufficed to
show that all peoples of all races, in the same
stage of their development, have showed the
same characteristics; in Europe, Thessalians,
Apulians, Campanians, Germans, Poles, etc.
Meanwhile the Celts, and specifically the
French, in different stages of their development, have showed quite different traits of
character. The psychology belongs to the
stage of development, not to the race!

Whenever, on the other hand, the religious
sanctions of the "state" are weak, or become so,
there develops as a group theory on the part of
the subjects, the concept, either clear or
blurred, of *Natural Law.* The lower class regards the race pride and the assumed superiority of the nobles as presumptuous, claims to
be of as good race and blood as the ruling
class—and from their standpoint again quite
correctly, since according to their views, labor,
efficiency and order are accounted the only
virtues. They are skeptical also as to the re-

ligion which is the helper of their adversaries;
and are as firmly convinced as are the nobles of
the directly opposite opinion, namely, that the
(privileges of the master group violate law as
well as reason.) Later development is not able
to add any essential point to the factors originally given.

Under the influence of these ideas, now
clearly, now obscurely brought out, the two
groups henceforth fight out their battles, each
for its own interests. The young state would
be burst apart under the strain of such centrifugal forces, were it not for the centripetal
pull of common interests, of the still more
powerful state-consciousness. The pressure
of foreigners from without, of common enemies, overcomes the inner strain of conflicting class interests. An example may be found
in the tale of the secession of the "Plebs" and
the successful mission of Menenius Agrippa.
And so the young state would, like a planet,
swing through all eternity in its predetermined
orbit, in accordance with the parallelogram of
forces, were it not that it and its surrounding

world is changed and developed until it produces new external and inner energies.

(d) THE PRIMITIVE FEUDAL STATE OF HIGHER GRADE

Growth in itself conditions important changes; and the young state must grow. The same forces that brought it into being, urge its extension, require it to grasp more power. Even were such a young state "sated," as many a modern state claims to be, it would still be forced to stretch and grow under penalty of extinction. Under primitive social conditions Goethe's lines apply with absolute truth: "You must rise or fall, conquer or yield, be hammer or anvil."

States are maintained in accordance with the same principles that called them into being. The primitive state is the creation of warlike robbery; and only by warlike robbery can it be preserved.

The economic want of the master group has no limits; no man is sufficiently rich to satisfy his desires. The political means are turned on

new groups of peasants not yet subjected, or
new coasts yet unpilfered are sought out. The
primitive state expands, until a collision takes
place on the edge of the "sphere of interests"
of another primitive state, which itself originated in precisely the same way. Then we
have for the first time, in place of the warlike robbery heretofore carried on, true war
in its narrower sense, since henceforth equally
organized and disciplined masses are hurled at
one another.

The object of the contest remains always
the same, the produce of the economic means
of the working classes, such as loot, tribute,
taxes and ground rent; but the contest no
longer takes place between a group intent on
exploiting and another mass to be exploited,
but between two master groups for the possession of the entire booty.

The final result of the conflict, in nearly all
instances, is the amalgamation of both primitive states into a greater. This in turn,
naturally and by force of the same causes,
reaches beyond its borders, devours its smaller

neighbors, and is perhaps in its turn devoured by some greater state.

The subjected laboring group may not take much interest in the final issue of these contests for the mastery; it is a matter of indifference whether it pays tribute to one or the other set of lords.   Their chief interest lies in the course of the particular fight, which is, in any case, paid for with their own hides. Therefore, except in cases of gross ill treatment and exploitation, the lower classes are rightly governed by their "state-consciousness" when, with all their might they aid their hereditary master group in times of war.   For if their master group is vanquished, the subjects suffer most severely from the utter devastation of war.   They fight literally for wife and children, for home and hearth, when they fight to prevent the rule of foreign masters.

The master group is involved completely in the issue of this fight for dominion.   In extreme cases, it may be completely exterminated, as were the local nobility of the Ger-

manic tribes in the Frankish Empire. Nearly
as bad, if not worse, is the prospect of being
thrust into the group of the serfs. Sometimes a well-timed treaty of peace preserves
their social position as master groups of subordinate rank: e. g., the Saxon nobility in
Norman England, or the Suppans in German territory taken from the Slavs. In other
cases, where the forces are about equal, the
two groups amalgamate into one master group
with equal rights, which forms a nobility whose
members intermarry. This, for instance, was
the situation in the Slavic Territories, where
isolated Wendish chieftains were treated as
the equals of the Germans, or in mediæval
Rome, in the case of prominent families from
the Alban Hills and Tuscany.

In this new "primitive feudal state of higher
grade," as we shall call it, the ruling group
may, therefore, disintegrate into a number of
more or less powerful and privileged strata.
The organization may show many varieties
because of the well-known fact, that often the
master group separates into two subordinated

economic and social layers, developed as we saw them in the herdsmen stage: the owners of large herds and of many slaves, and the ordinary freemen. Possibly the less complete differentiation into social ranks in the states created by huntsmen in the new world, is to be assigned to the circumstance that in the absence of herds, the concomitants of that form of ownership, and the original separation into classes, were not introduced into the state. We shall, later, see what force was exerted on the political and economic development of states in the old world by the differences in rank and property of the two strata of rulers.

Similarly, as in the case of the ruling group, a corresponding process of differentiation divides the subject group in the "primitive feudal state of a higher grade" into various strata more or less despised and compelled to render service. It is only necessary to recall the very marked difference in the social and jural position occupied by the peasantry in the Doric States, Lacedæmon and Crete, and among the Thessalians, where the perioiki had clear

rights of possession and fairly well protected
political rights, while the helots, in the latter
case the *penestai*, were almost unprotected in
life and property.   Among the old Saxons also
we find a class, the liti, intermediate between
the common freemen and the serfs.[52]   These
examples could be multiplied; apparently they
are caused by the same tendencies that brought
about the differentiation among the nobility
mentioned above.   When two primitive feudal
states amalgamate, their social layers stratify
in a variety of ways, which to a certain extent
are comparable to the combinations resulting
from mixing together two packs of cards.

It is certain that this mechanical mixture
caused by political forces, influences the development of *castes*, that is to say, of hereditary
professions, which at the same time form a
hierarchy of social classes. "Castes are
usually, if not always, consequences of conquest and subjugation by foreigners." [53]   Although this problem has not been completely
solved, it may be said that the formation of
castes has been very strongly influenced by

economic and religious factors. It is probable that castes came about in some such way as this: state-forming forces penetrated into existing economic organizations, and vocations underwent adaptation, and then became petrified under the influence of religious concepts, which, however, may also have influenced their original formation. This seems to follow from the fact that even as between man and woman there exist certain separations of vocation, which, so to say, are taboo and impassable. Thus among all huntsmen, tilling the ground is woman's work, while among many African shepherds, as soon as the ox-plow is used, agriculture becomes man's work, and then women may not, under pain of sacrilege, use the domestic cattle.*

It is likely that such religious concepts may have brought it about that a vocation became hereditary, and then compulsorily hereditary, especially where a tribe or a village carried on

---

* Similarly there are North Asiatic tribes of huntsmen, where women are definitely forbidden to touch the hunting gear or to cross a hunting trail.—Ratzel I, page 650.

a particular craft. This happens with all
tribes in a state of nature, where intercourse
is easily possible, especially in the case of
islanders. When some such group has been
conquered by another tribe, the subjects, with
their developed hereditary vocations, tend to
form within the new state entity a pure
"caste." Their caste position depends partly
upon the esteem they had heretofore enjoyed
among their own people, and partly upon the
advantage which their vocation affords their
new masters. If, as was often the case, waves
of conquest followed one another in series, the
formation of castes might be multiplied, especially if in the meantime economic development had worked out many vocational classes.

This development is probably best seen in
the group of smiths, who, in nearly all cases,
have occupied a peculiar position, half feared
and half despised. In Africa especially, since
the beginning of time, we find tribes of expert
smiths, as followers and dependents of shepherd tribes. The Hyksos brought such tribes
with them into the Nile country, and perhaps

owed their decisive victory to arms made by them; and until recent times the Dinka kept the iron working Djur in a sort of subject relation.   The same applied also to the nomads of the Sahara; while our northern sagas are filled with the tribal contrast to the "dwarfs" and the fear of their magical powers.   All the elements were at hand in a developed state for the formation of sharply differentiated castes.[54]

How the coöperation of religious concepts affects the beginning of these formations may be well illustrated by an example from Polynesia.   Here, "although many natives have the ability to do ship-building, only one privileged class may exercise the craft, so closely is the interest of the states and the societies bound up in this art.   All over the archipelago formerly, and to this day in Fiji, the carpenters, who are almost exclusively ship-builders, form a special caste, bear the high sounding title of 'the king's workmen,' and enjoy the prerogative of having their own chieftains. . . . Everything is done in accordance with ancient tradition; the laying the keel, the completion of the ship, and the launching, all take place amidst religious ceremonies and feasts." [55]

Where superstition has been strongly developed, a genuine system of castes may come about, based partly on economic and partly on ethnic foundations. In Polynesia, for example, the articulation of the classes, through the operation of the taboo, has brought about a state of affairs very like a most thorough-going caste system.[56]   Similar results may be seen in Southern Arabia.[57]   It is unnecessary at this place to enlarge on the important place which religion had in the origin and maintenance of separate castes in ancient Egypt and in modern India.*

These are the elements of the primitive feudal state of higher grade. They are more manifold and more numerous than in the lower

---

* Besides, it seems that the rigidity of the Indian caste-system is not so harsh in practise. The guild seems as often to break through the barriers of caste as the converse.—Ratzel II, page 596.

primitive state; but in both, legal constitution and political-economic distributon are fundamentally the same. The products of the economic means are still the object of the group struggle. This remains now as ever the moving impulse of the domestic policy of the state, while the political means continues now as ever to constitute the moving impulse of its foreign policy in attack or in defense. Identical group theories continue to justify, both for the upper classes and the lower, the objects and means of external and domestic struggles.

But the development can not remain stationary. Growth differs from mere increase in bulk; growth means a constantly heightening differentiation and integration.

The farther the primitive feudal state extends its dominion, the more numerous its subjects, and the denser its population, the more there develops a political-economic division of labor, which calls forth new needs and new means of supplying them; and the more there come into sharp contrasts the distinctions of economic, and consequently of social, class strata, in accordance with what I have called the "law of the agglomeration about existing nuclei of wealth." [This growing differentiation becomes decisive for the further development of the primitive feudal state, and still more for its conclusion.

This conclusion is not meant to be, in any sense, the physical end of such a state. We do not mean the death of a state, whereby such a feudal state of the higher type disappears, in consequence of conflict with a more powerful state, either on the same or on a higher plane of development, as was the case of the Mogul states of India or of Uganda in their conflicts with Great Britain. Neither does it mean such a stagnation as that into which Persia and Turkey have fallen, which represents for a time only a pause in development, since these countries, either of their own force or by foreign conquest, must soon be pushed on the way of their destiny. Neither have we meant the rigidity of the gigantic Chinese Empire, which can last only so long as foreign powers refrain from forcing its mysterious gates.*

The outcome here spoken of means the further development of the primitive feudal state, a matter of importance to our understanding of universal history as a *process*. The principal lines of development into which this issue branches off are twofold and of fundamentally different character. *But this polar opposition is conditioned by a like contrast between two sorts of economic wealth each of which increases in accordance with the "law of agglomeration about existing nuclei."* In the one case, it is movable property; in the other, landed property. Here it is the capital of commerce, there property in land,

---

* Had we the space, a detailed exposition of this exceptional development of a feudal state would be tempting. China would be well worth a more detailed discussion, since, in many aspects it has approached the condition of "free citizenship" more closely than any people of Western Europe. China has overcome the consequences of the feudal system more thoroughly than we Europeans have; and has made, early in its development, the great property interests in the land harmless, so that their bastard offspring, capitalism, hardly came into being; while in addition, it has worked out to a considerable degree the problems of coöperative production and of coöperative distribution.

accumulating in the hands of a smaller and smaller number, and thereby overturning radically the articulation of classes, and with it the whole State.

The maritime State is the scene of the development of movable wealth; the territorial State is the embodiment of the development of landed property. The final issue of the first is *capitalistic exploitation* by slavery, the outcome of the latter is, first of all, the *developed feudal State.*

Capitalistic exploitation by slavery, the typical result of the development of the so-called "antique States" on the Mediterranean, does not end in the death of states, which is of no importance, but in the death of peoples, because of the consumption of population. In the pedigree of the historical development of the State, it forms a side branch, from which no further immediate growth can take place.

The developed feudal State, however, represents the principal branch, the continuation of the trunk; and is therefore the origin for the further growth of the State. Thence it has developed into the State governed by feudal systems; into absolutism; into the modern constitutional State; and if we are right in our prognosis, it will become a "free citizenship."

So long as the trunk grew only in one direction, i. e., to include the primitive feudal State of higher grade, our sketch of its growth and development could and did comprise both forms. Henceforth, after the bifurcation, our story branches and follows each branch to its last twig.

We begin, then, with the maritime states, although they are not the older form. On the contrary, as far back as the dawn of history clears the fog of prehistoric existence, the first strong states were formed as territorial states, which then, by their own powers, attained the scale of developed feudal States. But beyond this stage, at least as regards those States most interesting to our culture, most of them either remained stationary or fell into the power of maritime states; and then, infected with the deadly poison of capitalistic exploitation through slavery, were destroyed by the same plague.

The further progress of the expanded feudal states of higher grade could take place only after the maritime states had run their course: mighty forms of domination and statescraft these became, and they subsequently influenced and furthered the conformation of the territorial states that grew from their ruins.

For that reason the story of the fate of maritime states must be first traced, as these are the introduction to the higher forms of state life. After first tracing the lateral branch, we shall then return to the starting point, the primitive feudal State, follow the main trunk to the development of the modern constitutional State, and anticipating actual history, sketch the "free citizenship" of the future.

CHAPTER IV

THE MARITIME STATE

THE course of life and the path of suffering of the State founded by sea nomads, as has been stated above, is determined by commercial capital; just as that of the territorial State is determined by capital vested in realty; and, we may add, that of the modern constitutional State by productive capital. The sea nomad, however, did not invent trade or merchandising, fairs or markets or cities; these preëxisted, and since they served his purpose, were now developed to suit his interests. All these institutions, serving the economic means, the barter for equivalents, had long since been discovered.

Here for the first time in our survey we find the economic means not the object of exploitation by the political means, but as a coöperating agent in originating the State, one might call it the "chain" passing into the "lift" created by the feudal state to bring forth a more elaborate structure. The genesis of the maritime State would not be thoroughly intelligible, were we not to premise a statement concerning traffic and interchange of wares in prehistoric times. Furthermore, no prognosis of the modern state is complete, which does not take into account the independently formed economic means of aboriginal barter.

(a) TRAFFIC IN PREHISTORIC TIMES

The psychological explanation of barter has brought forth the theory of the marginal utility, its greatest merit. According to this theory, the subjective valuation of any economic good decreases in proportion to the number of objects of the same kind possessed by the same owner. When even two proprietors meet, each having a number of similar articles, they will gladly barter, provided political means are barred, i. e., if both parts are apparently equally strong and well-armed, or in the very early stage, are within the sacred circle of relationship. By barter, each one receives property of very high subjective value, in place of property of very low subjective value, so that both parties are gainers in the transaction. The desire of primitive people for bartering must be stronger than that of cultured ones. For at this stage man does not value his own goods, but covets the things belonging to strangers, and is hardly affected by calculated economic considerations.

On the other hand, we must not forget that there are primitive peoples for whom barter has no attraction whatever. "Cook tells of tribes in Polynesia, with whom no intercourse was possible, since presents made absolutely no impression on them, and were afterward thrown away; everything shown them they regarded with indifference, and with no desire to own it, while with their own things they would not part; in fact, they had no conception of either trade or barter." [58]   So Westermarck is of the opinion that "barter and traffic are comparatively late inventions." In this he stands in opposition to Peschel, who would have it that man in the earliest known stage of development engaged in barter. Westermarck states that there is no proof "that the cave-dwellers of Périgord from the reindeer period obtained their rock-crystals, their shells from the Atlantic, and the horns of the Saiga antelope from (modern) Poland by way of barter." [59]

In spite of these exceptions, which admit other explanations—perhaps the natives feared sorcery—the history of primitive peoples shows that the desire to trade and barter is a universal human characteristic. It can, however, take effect only when these primitive men on meeting with strangers are offered new enticing objects, since in the immediate circle of their own blood kinsmen every one has the same kinds of property, and in their natural communism, on the average about the same amount.

Yet even then, barter, the beginning of all regular trading, can take place only when the meeting with foreigners is a peaceable one. But is there any possibility for peaceable meeting with foreigners? Is not primitive man, through his entire life, and especially at the period when barter begins, still under the apprehension that every one of a different horde is an enemy to be feared as the wolf?

After trade is developed, it is, as a rule, strongly influenced by the "political means," "trade generally follows robbery." [60] But its first beginnings are chiefly the result of the economic means, the outcome of pacific, not warlike, intercourse.

The international relations of primitive huntsmen with one another must not be confused with those existing either between the huntsmen or herdsmen and their peasants, or amongst the herdsmen themselves. There are, undoubtedly, blood-feuds, or feuds because of looted women, or possibly because of violation of the districts set aside for hunting grounds; but these lack that strong incentive, which is the consequence of avarice alone, of the desire to despoil other men of the products of their labor. Therefore, the "wars" of primitive huntsmen are scarcely real wars, but rather scuffles and single combats, carried on frequently—as are the German student duels —according to an established ceremonial, and prolonged only up to the point of incapacity to fight, as one might say, "until claret has been drawn." [61] These tribes, numerically very weak, wisely limit bloodshed to the indispensable amount—e. g., in case of a blood vendetta feud—and thus avoid starting new vendetta blood feuds.

For this reason, pacific relations with their neighbors on an equal economic scale are much stronger, and also freer from the incentive to use political means, both among huntsmen and among primitive peasants, than among herdsmen. There are numerous examples where the former meet peaceably to exploit natural resources in common. "While yet in primitive stages of civilization, great masses of people gather together, from time to time, at places where useful objects may be found. The Indians of a large part of America made regular pilgrimages to the flint grounds; others assembled annually at harvest time at

the Zizania swamps of the lakes of the Northwest. The Australians, living scattered in the
Barku district, assemble from all directions for
the harvest festivals at the swamp beds of
the corn bearing Marsiliacae. When the
bonga-bonga trees in Queensland produce a
superabundant crop, and a greater store is on
hand than the tribe can consume, foreign tribes
are permitted to share therein." [63] "Various
tribes agree on the common ownership of definite strips of territory, and likewise of the
quarries of phonolite for hatchets." [64] Numerous Australian tribes have common con-
sultations and sessions of the elders for judgment. In these, the remainder of the population form the bystanders, a custom similar to
the Germanic *"Umstand"* in the primitive folk-
moot.[65]

It is but natural that such meetings should
bring about barter. Perhaps this explains the
origin of those "weekly fairs held by the Negroes of Central Africa in the midst of the
primæval forest *under special arrangements
for the peace,"* [66] and likewise the great fairs,

said to be very ancient, of the fur hunters of
the extreme north of the Tschuktsche.

All these things presuppose the development
of pacific forms of intercourse between neighboring groups.   These forms are to be found
almost universally.   They could very easily be
developed at this period, since the discovery
had not yet been made that men can be utilized
as labor motors.   At this stage, the stranger is
treated as an enemy only in doubtful cases.
If he comes with apparently peaceable intent,
he is treated as a friend. : Therefore, a whole
code of public law ceremonies grew up, intended to demonstrate the pacific intent of the
newcomer.* ' One puts aside one's arms and
shows one's unarmed hand, or one sends heralds in advance, who are always inviolable.

It is clear that these forms represent some
kind of claim to hospitality, and in fact it is by
this guest-right that peaceful trade is first

* In this category must be reckoned the salutation, still
in use in some parts, "Peace Be With You."   It is expressive
of the perversity of Tolstoi's later years that he misappre-
hends this characteristic mark of a time when war was the
normal state of affairs, as the remnant of a golden age of
peace. *The Importance of the Russian Revolution* (German
translation by A. Hess, p. 17).

made possible. The exchange of guest-gifts precedes, and appears to introduce, barter proper. It becomes, therefore, important to investigate the source of hospitality.

Westermarck, in his recent monumental work (1907), *Origin and Development of Moral Concepts,*[68] states that the custom of hospitality results from two causes, curiosity for news from the stranger from afar, and still more from the fear that the stranger may be endowed with powers of sorcery, imputed to him just because he is a stranger.* In the Bible, hospitality is recommended for the reason that one can not know that the stranger may not be an angel. The superstitious race fears his curse (the Erinys of the Greeks) and hastens to propitiate the stranger. Having been accepted as a guest he is inviolable and enjoys the sacred right of the blood-related group, and is regarded as belonging to

* This may account for the use made of old women as heralds. They are doubly available for that purpose, since they are worthless for warfare, and are supposed to be endowed with specific powers of sorcery (Westermarck), even more than old men, who also are treated cautiously, since they may soon become "ghosts."

it during his stay. Therefore he partakes of
the benefits of the aboriginal communism
reigning in the group, and shares its property.
The host demands and receives whatever he
claims, the stranger obtains in turn what he
asks for. When the peaceable intercourse becomes more frequent, the mutual giving of
guest-presents may develop into a trading
arrangement, because the trader gladly returns to the spot where he found good enter-
tainment and a profitable exchange and where
he is protected by the laws of hospitality, instead of seeking new places, where, often with
danger to his life, he would first have to acquire
the right to hospitality.

The existence of an "international" division
of labor is, of course, presupposed before the
development of a regular trade relation can
begin. Such a division of labor exists much
earlier and to a greater extent than is generally believed. "It is quite erroneous to sup-
pose that the division of labor takes place only
on a high scale of economic development.
There are in the interior of Africa villages of

iron-smiths, nay, of such as only turn out dart-knives; New Guinea has its villages of potters, North America its arrow-head makers." [69] From such specialties there develops trade, whether through roving merchants, or by gifts to one's hosts, or by peace-gifts from tribe to tribe. In North America, the Kaddu trade in bows. "Obsidian was universally employed for arrow heads and knives; on the Yellowstone, on the Snake River, in New Mexico, but especially in Mexico. Thence the precious article was distributed all over the entire country as far as Ohio and Tennessee, a distance of nearly two thousand miles." [70]

According to Vierkandt: "From the purely home-made products of primitive peoples, there results a system of trade totally distinct from that prevailing under modern conditions. . . . Each separate tribe has developed special aptitudes, leading to interexchange. Even among the comparatively uncivilized Indian tribes of South America, we find such differentiations. . . . By such a trade, products may be distributed over extra-

ordinary distances, not in any direct way
through professional traders, but through a
gradual passing along from tribe to tribe.
The origin of such a trade, as Buecher has
shown, is to be traced back to the exchange of
guest-gifts." [71]

Besides this exchange of guest-gifts, a trade
may grow from the peace offerings which adversaries after a fight exchange as a sign of
reconciliation. Sartorius reports on Polynesia: "After a war between different
islands, the peace offerings for each group
were something novel; and if the present and
return present pleased both parties, a repeti-
tion took place, and thus again the way for
exchange of products was opened. But, these,
in contrast to guest-gifts, were the bases of
continuing intercourse. Here, in place of the
contact of individuals, tribes and peoples met.
Women are the first object of barter; they
form the connecting link between strange
tribes, and according to evidence from many
sources, women are exchanged for cattle." [72]

We meet here an object of trade, exchangeable even without "international division of labor." And it appears as though the *exchange of women* had, in many ways, smoothed the way for the traffic in merchandise, as though it had been the first step toward the *peaceable* integration of tribes, which accompanied the *warlike* integration of the formation of the State. Lippert, however, believes that the peaceful *exchange of fire* antedates this barter.[73] Conceding that this custom is very ancient, he can nevertheless trace it only from rudiments of observances and of law; and since proof is no longer accessible, we shall not pursue the question further in this place.

On the other hand, the exchange of women is observed universally, and doubtless exerts an extraordinarily strong influence in the development of peaceable intercourse between neighboring tribes, and in the preparation for barter of merchandise. The story of the Sabine women, who threw themselves between their brothers and their husbands, as these were about to engage in battle, must have been an actuality in a thousand instances in the course

of the development of the human race. All
over the world, the marriage of near relatives
is considered an outrage, as "incest," for
reasons not within the scope of this book.[74]
This directs the sexual longing toward the
women of neighboring tribes, and thus makes
the loot of women a part of the primary inter-
tribal relations; and in nearly all cases, unless
strong feelings of race counteract it, the violent
carrying off of women is gradually commuted
to barter and purchase, the custom resulting
from the relative undesirability of the women
of one's own blood in comparison to the wives
to be had from other tribes.

Where division of labor made at all possible
the exchange of goods, the relations among the
various tribes would thereafter be made serv-
iceable to it; the exogamic groups gradually
become accustomed regularly to meet on a
peaceful basis. The peace, originally protecting the horde of blood relations, thereafter
comes to be extended over a wider circle. One
example from numberless instances: "Each
of the two Camerun tribes has its own 'bush

countries,' places where its own tribesmen trade, and where, by intermarriage, they have relatives. Here also exogamy shows its tribe-linking power."

These are the principal lines of growth of peaceful barter and traffic; from the right to hospitality and the exchange of women, perhaps also from the exchange of fire, to the trade in commodities. In addition to this, markets and fairs, and perhaps also traders, were almost uniformly regarded as being under the protection of a god who preserved peace and avenged its violation. Thus we have brought the fundamentals of this most important sociological factor to the point where the political means enters as a cause to disturb, rearrange, and then to develop and affect the creations of the economic means.

(b) TRADE AND THE PRIMITIVE STATE

There are two very important reasons why the robber-warrior should not unduly interfere with such markets and fairs as he may find within his conquered domain.

The first, which is extra-economic, is the superstitious fear that the godhead will avenge a breach of the peace. The second, which is economic, and probably is the more important —and I think I am the first to point out this connection—is that the conquerors can not well do without the markets.

The booty of the primitive victors consists of much property which is unavailable for their immediate use and consumption. Since valuable articles at that period exist in but few forms, while these few occur in large quantity, the "marginal utility" of any one kind is held very low. This applies especially to the most important product of the political means, slaves. Let us first take up the case of the herdsman: his need of slaves is limited by the size of his herds; he is very likely to exchange his surplus for other objects of greater value to him: for salt, ornaments, arms, metals, woven materials, utensils, etc. For that reason, the herdsman is not only at all times a robber, always in addition he is a merchant and trader and he protects trade.

He protects trade coming his way in order to exchange his loot against the products of another civilization—from the earliest times, nomads have convoyed the caravans passing through their steppes or deserts in consideration of protection money—but he also protects trade even in places conquered by him in prehistoric times. Quite the same sort of consideration which influenced the herdsmen to change from bear stage to bee-keeper stage, must have influenced them to maintain and protect ancient markets and fairs. One single looting, in this case, would mean killing the hen that lays the golden eggs. It is more profitable to preserve the market and rather to extend the prevailing peace over it, since there is not only the profit to be had from an exchange of foreign wares against loot, but also the protection money, the lords' toll, to be collected. For that reason princes of feudal states of every stage of development extended over markets, highways and merchants, their especial protection, the "king's peace," often indeed reserving to themselves the monopoly of foreign trade. Everywhere we see them busily engaged in calling into being new fairs and cities by the grant of protection and immunity.

This interest in the system of fairs and markets makes it thoroughly credible that tribes of herdsmen respected existing market places in their sphere of influence to such an extent that they suspended the exertion of the political means so completely as not even to exercise "dominion" over them. The story told by Herodotus is inherently probable, though he was astonished that the Argippæans had a sacred market amidst the lawless Scythian herdsmen, and that their unarmed inhabitants were effectively protected through the hallowed peace of their market place. Many similar phenomena make this the more easily believable.

"No one dare harm them, since they are considered *holy;* and yet they have no arms; but it is they who allay the quarrels of their neighbors, and whoever has escaped to them as a runaway may not be touched by any other man." [76] Similar instances are found frequently: "It is always the same story of the Argippæans, the story of the 'holy,' 'unarmed,' 'just,' bartering, and strife-settling tribelet in the midst of a Bedouin-like, nomadic population." [77] Cære may be taken as an example of a higher type. Strabo says of its inhabitants: "The Greeks thought highly of their bravery and justice, because although powerful in a great degree, they abstained from robbery." Mommsen, who quotes this passage, adds: "This does not exclude piracy, which was engaged in by the merchants of Cære as well as by all other merchants, but rather that Cære was a sort of free harbor for the Phœnicians as for the Greeks." [78]

Cære is not like the fair of the Argippæans, a market place in the interior of a district of land nomads, but is in the midst of *a domain of sea nomads, a port endowed with its own peace.* [79] This is one of those typical formations whose importance, in my estimation, has not been appreciated at its real value. They have, it seems to me, exercised a mighty influence on the genesis of maritime states.

Those reasons by which we saw the land nomads forced to preserve, if not to create, market places, must with even more intensity, have coerced the sea nomads to similar demeanor. For the transportation of loot, especially of herds and of slaves, is difficult and dangerous on the trails across the desert or the steppes: the slow progress invites pursuit. But with war-canoe and "dragon-ship" this transportation is easy and safe. For that reason, the Viking is even much more a trader and merchant than is the herdsman. As is said in *Faust*, "War, Commerce, and Piracy are inseparable."

(c) THE GENESIS OF THE MARITIME STATE

In many cases, I believe, trade in the loot of piracy is the origin of those cities around which, as political centers, the city-states of the antique or Mediterranean civilization grew up; while in very many other cases, the same trade coöperated to bring them to the same point of political development.

These harbor markets developed from probably two general types: they grew up either as piratical fortresses directly and intentionally placed in hostile territory, or else as "merchant colonies" based on treaty rights in the harbors of foreign primitive or developed feudal states.

Of the first type, we have a number of important examples from ancient history which correspond exactly to the fourth stage of our scheme, where an armed colony of pirates plants itself down at a commercially and strategically defendable point on the seacoast of a foreign state. The most notable instance is Carthage; and in like manner, the Greek sea nomads, Ionians, Dorians and Achæans, settled in their sea castles on the Adriatic and Tyrrhenian coasts of Southern Italy, on the islands of these seas, and on the gulfs of Southern Gaul. Phœnicians, Etruscans,* Greeks,

---

* Whether the Etruscans were immigrants into Italy by land who took up piracy after having made war successfully on land, or whether as sea nomads they had already settled the

and according to modern investigation, Carians, all about the Mediterranean, founded their "States" after the same type, with identical class division into masters and servile peasantry of the neighboring territory.[79]

Some of these states on the coast developed into feudal states of the type of the territorial states; and the master class then became a landed aristocracy. The factors in this change were: first, geographical conditions, lack of good harbors, and a wide stretch of *hinterland* cultivated by peaceful peasants; and secondly, very probably, the acquired organization into classes taken with them from their original homes. In many cases, they were fugitive nobles, the vanquished of domestic feuds, or younger sons, sometimes an entire generation of youth of both sexes, who thus started "on the viking," and having at home had lands and serfs, as petty lords, they again sought in foreign lands what they regarded as their due. The occupation of England by the Anglo-

country along the sea named after them, has not been determined.

Saxons, and of Southern Italy by the Normans, are examples of this method; so too are the Spanish and Portuguese colonizations of Mexico and of South America. The Achæan colonies of Greater Greece in Southern Italy furnish additional and very important instances of this development of territorial feudal states by sea nomads: "This Achæan League of cities was a true colonization. The cities were without harbors—Croton only had a fair roadstead—*and were without any trade of their own;* the Sybarite could boast of his growing gray in his water town between his home bridges, while buying and selling were carried on by Milesians and Etruscans. On the other hand, the Greeks in this region not only controlled the fringe of the shore, but ruled from sea to sea; . . . the native agricultural inhabitants were forced into a relation of clientage or serfdom, and were required to work the farms of their masters or to pay tribute to them." [80] It is probable that most of the Doric colonies in Crete were similarly organized.

But in the course of universal history these "territorial states," whether they arose more or less frequently, did not acquire any such importance as did those maritime cities which devoted their principal energies to commerce and to privateering. Mommsen contrasts in distinct and well chosen sentences the Achæan landed squire with the "royal merchants" of the Greek Colonies in Southern Italy: "In no way did they spurn agriculture or the increase of territory; the Greeks were not satisfied, at least not after they became powerful, to remain within the confined space of a fortified commercial factory in the midst of the country of the barbarians, as the Phœnicians had done. Their cities were founded primarily and exclusively for purposes of trade, and unlike the Achæan colonies, were universally situated at the best harbors and landing places." [81] We are certain, in the case of the Ionic colonies, and may well assume it for the other cases, that the founders of these cities were not landed squires, but seafaring merchants.

But such maritime states or cities, in the

strict sense, came into being not only through warlike conquest, but also through peaceable beginnings, by a more or less mixed *pénétration pacifique.*

Where, however, the Vikings did not meet peaceable peasants, but feudal states in the primitive stage, willing to fight, they offered and accepted terms of peace and settled down as colonies of merchants.

We know of such cases from every part of the world, in harbors and on markets held on shore. To take the instances with which Germans are most conversant, there are the settlements of North German merchants in countries along the German ocean and the Baltic Sea, the German Steel Yard in London, the Hansa in Sweden and Norway, on the Island of Schönen, and in Russia, at Novgorod. In Wilna, the capital of the Grand Dukes of Lithuania, there was such a colony; and the Fondaco dei Tedeschi in Venice is another example of a similar institution. The strangers in nearly every instance settle down as a compact mass, subject to their own laws and their own jurisdiction. They often acquire great political influence, sometimes extending to dominion over the state. One would think the following tale of Ratzel, concerning the coast and islands of the Indian Ocean, were a contemporaneous narrative of the Phœnician or Greek invasion of the Mediterranean at about 1,000 B. C.: "Whole nations have, so to say, been liquefied by trade, especially the proverbially clever, zealous, omnipresent Malays of Sumatra; as well as the treacherous Bugi of Celebes. These can be met with at every place from Singapore to New Guinea. Latterly, especially in Borneo, they have immigrated in masses on the call of the Borneo chieftains. Their influence was so strong that they were permitted *to govern themselves according to their own laws,* and they felt themselves so strong *that repeatedly they attempted to achieve independence.* The Achinese formerly occupied a similar position. Malacca had been made the principal mart by Malays from Sumatra, and after its decline, Achin became the most frequented harbor of

this distant east, especially for the first quarter
of the seventeenth century, the pivotal period
of the development of that corner of the
world." [82] The following, from among numberless instances, demonstrate the universality
of this form of settlement: "In Urga, *where
they politically dominate,* the merchants are
crowded together into a separate Chinese
Town." [83] In the Jewish States there were
"small colonies of foreign merchants and mechanics, set apart in distinct quarters of the
cities. Here, under the king's protection, they
could live according to their own religious customs." [84] We may also compare with this,
First Kings XX, 34. "King Omri of Ephraim
was forced by the military success of his opponent, the King of Damascus, to grant to the
Aramaic merchants the use of certain parts of
the city of Samaria, where under royal protection they could trade. Later, when the turn of
war favored his successor, Ahab, the latter demanded the same privilege for the Ephraimitic
merchants in Damascus." [85] "The inhabitants
of Italy, wherever they were, held together as

solid and organized masses, the soldiers as legionaries, the merchants of all large cities as
corporations; while the Roman citizens domiciled or dwelling in the various provincial *cir-
cuits,* were organized as a 'convention of
Roman citizens' with their own communal government." [86] We may recall the mediæval
Ghettos, which, before the great persecution of
the Jews in the Middle Ages, were similar
merchant colonies. The settlements of Europeans in the ports of strong foreign empires
at the present time show similar corporate organizations, having their own constitution and
(consular) jurisdiction. China, Turkey and
Morocco must continue to bear this mark of
inferiority, while recently Japan has been able
to rid herself of that badge.

The most interesting point about these colonies, at least for our study, consists in their
general tendency to extend their political
influence into complete domination. And
there is good reason for this. Merchants have
a mass of movable wealth, which is likely to be
used as a decisive factor in the political up-

heavals constantly disturbing all feudal states, be it in international wars between two neighboring states, or in intra-national fights, such as wars of succession. In addition to this the colonists, in many cases, may rely on the power of their home state, basing their claim on ties of blood and on uncommonly strong commercial interests; while there is besides, the fact that in many cases they have in their warlike sailor-folk and their numerous slaves an effective and compact force of their own, capable of accomplishing much in a limited sphere.

The following story of the rôle played by Arab merchants in East Africa appears to me to show a historical type heretofore not sufficiently appreciated: "When Speke, as the first European, made this trip in 1857, the Arabs were merchants, living as aliens in the land. When in 1861 he passed the same way, the Arabs resembled great landed proprietors with rich estates and were waging war with the native territorial ruler. This process, repeatedly found in many other regions in the

interior of Africa, is the necessary consequence
of the balance of power. The foreign merchants, be they Arabs or Suaheli, ask the privilege of transit and pay tribute for it; they
establish warehouses, which the chiefs favor,
as these seem both to satisfy their vanity and
to extend their connections; then incurring the
suspicion, oppression and persecution of the
chiefs, the merchants refuse to pay the rack
tolls and dues, which have grown with their
increased prosperity. At last, in one of the
inevitable fights for the succession, the Arabs
take the side of one pretender if he is pliable
enough, and are thus brought into internal
quarrels of the country and take part in the
often endless wars." [87]

This political activity of the merchant denizens (*metoikoi*) is a constantly recurring type.
"In Borneo there developed from the settlements of Chinese gold diggers separate
states." [88] Properly speaking, the entire history of colonization by Europeans is a series
of examples of the law that, with any superior
force, the factories and larger settlements of

foreigners tend to grow into domination, unless they approximate to the primal type of simple piracy, such as the Spanish and Portuguese conquests, or the East India Companies, both the English and the Dutch. "There lies a robber state beside the ocean, between the Rhine and the Scheldt," are the accusing words of the Dutch Multatuli. All East Asiatic, American and African colonies of all European peoples arose as one or the other of these two types.

But the aliens do not always obtain unconditional mastery. Sometimes the host state is too strong, and the newcomers remain politically powerless but protected aliens; as, for example, the Germans in England. Sometimes the host state, although subjugated, becomes strong enough to shake off the foreign domination; so, for instance, Sweden drove out the Hanseats who had imposed on her their sovereignty. In some cases, a conqueror overcomes both merchants and host state, and subjugates both; as happened to the republics of Novgorod and Pskov, when the Russians annexed them. In many cases, however, the rich foreigners and the domestic nobility amalgamate into one group of rulers, following the type of the formation of territorial states, in which we saw this take place whenever two about equally strong groups of rulers came into conflict. It seems to me that this last named situation is the most probable assumption for the genesis of the most important city states of antiquity, for the Greek maritime cities, and for Rome.

Of Greek history, to use the terms of Kurt Breysig, we know only the "Middle Ages," of Roman history, only its "Modern Times." For the matters that preceded, we must be extremely careful in drawing deductions from fancied analogies. But it seems to me that enough facts are proved and admitted to permit the conclusion that Athens, Corinth, Mycenæ, Rome, etc., became states in the manner already set forth. And this would follow, even if the data from all known demography and general history were not of such universal validity as to permit the conclusion in itself.

We know accurately from the names of places (Salamis: Island of Peace, equivalent to Market-Island), from the names of heroes, from monuments, and from immediate tradition, that in many Greek harbors there existed Phœnician factories, while the *hinterland* was occupied by small feudal states with the typical articulation of nobles, common freemen, and slaves. It can not seriously be disputed that the development of the city states was powerfully advanced by foreign influences; and this is true, though no specific evidence can be adduced to show that any of the Phœnician, or of the still more powerful Carian merchants were either allowed to intermarry with the families of the resident nobility, or were made full citizens, or finally even became princes.

The same applies to Rome, concerning which Mommsen, a cautious author, states: "Rome owes its importance, if not its origin, to these commercial and strategic relations. Evidence of this is found in many traces of far greater value than the tales of historical novels pretending to be authentic. Take an instance of the primæval relations existing between Rome and Cære, which was for Etruria what Rome was for Latium, and thereafter was its nearest neighbor and commercial friend; or the uncommon importance attributed to the bridge over Tiber and the bridge building (Pontifex Maximus) in every part of the Roman State; or the galley in the municipal coat of arms. To this source may be traced the primitive Roman harbor dues to which, from early times, only those goods were subject which were intended for sale (*promercale*) and not what entered the harbor of Ostia, for the proper use of the charterer (*usuarium*), and which constituted therefore an impost on trade. For that reason we find the comparatively early use of minted money, and the commercial treaties of states oversea with Rome. In this sense, then, Rome may, as the story of its origin states, have been rather a created than a developed city, and among the Latin cities rather the youngest than the eldest." [89]

It would require the work of a lifetime of historical research to investigate these possibilities, or rather these probabilities; and then to write the constitutional history of these pre-ëminently important city states, and to draw thence the very necessary conclusions. It seems to me that along this path there would be found much information on many an obscure question, such as the Etruscan dominion in Rome, or the origin of the rich families of Plebeians, or concerning the Athenian *metoikoi,* and many other problems.

Here we can only follow the thread which holds out the hope of leading us through the labyrinth of historical tradition to the issue.

(d) ESSENCE AND ISSUE OF THE MARITIME STATES

All these are true "States" in the sociologic sense, whether they arose from the fortresses of sea-robbers, or from harbors of original land nomads as merchant colonies which obtained dominion or which amalgamated with the dominating group of the host people. For they are nothing but the organization of the political means, their form is domination, their con-

tent the economic exploitation of the subject
by the master group.

So far as the principle is concerned, they
are not to be differentiated from the States
founded by land nomads; and yet they have
taken a different form, both from internal and
external reasons, and show a different psychology of classes.

One must not believe that class feeling was
at all different in these and in the territorial
states. Here as there the master class looks
down with the same contempt on the subjects,
on the *"Rantuses,"* on the "man with the blue
fingernails," as the German patrician in the
Middle Ages looked on a being with whom,
even when free born, no intermarriage or
social intercourse was permitted. Little indeed does the class theory of the *καλο-
κάγαθοι* (well-born) or of the patricians
(children of ancestors) differ from that of the
country squires. But other circumstances
here bring about differences, consonant,
naturally, with class interests. In any district
ruled by merchants, highway robbery can not

be tolerated, and therefore it is considered, e. g., among the maritime Greeks, a vulgar crime. The tale of Theseus would not in a territorial state have been pointed against the highwaymen. On the other hand, "piracy was regarded by them, in most remote times, as a trade nowise dishonorable ̧ . . of which ample proof may be found in the Homeric poems; while at a much later period Polycrates had organized a well developed robber-state on the Island of Samos." "In the *Corpus Juris*, mention is made of a law of Solon in which the association of pirates (ἐπὶ λείαν οἰχόμενοι) is recognized as a permissible company." [90]

But quite apart from such details, mentioned only because they serve to cast a clear light on the growth of the "ideologic superstructure," * the basic conditions of existence of maritime states, utterly different from those of territorial states, called into being two exceedingly important phenomena, which are of

---

* How characteristic of these relations it is that Great Britain, the only "maritime state" of Europe, even at this present day will not surrender the right to arm privateers.

universal historical importance, viz., the
growth of a *democratic constitution,* whereby
the gigantic contest between the sultanism of
the Orient and the civic freedom of the West
was to be fought out (according to Mommsen
the true content of universal history) ; and in
the second place the development of *capitalistic slave-work,* which in the end was to anni-
hilate all these states.

Let us first consider the inner or socio-psychological causes of this contrast between the
territorial and the maritime state. States are maintained by the same principle
from which they arise. Conquest of land and
populations is the *ratio essendi* of a territorial
state; and by the repeated conquest of lands
and populations it must grow, until its natural
growth is checked by mountain ranges, desert,
or ocean, or its sociological bounds are determined by contact with other states of its
own kind, which it can not subjugate. The
maritime state, on the other hand, came into
being from piracy and trade; and through
these two means, it must strive to extend its

power. For this purpose, no extended territory need be absolutely subjected to its sway. There is no need to carry its development beyond the first five stages. The maritime states rarely, and only when compelled, proceed beyond the fifth stage, and attain to complete intra-nationality and amalgamation. Usually, it is enough if other sea nomads and traders are kept away, if the monopoly of robbery and trade is secured, and if the "subjects" are kept quiet by forts and garrisons. Important places of production are, of course, actually "dominated"; and this applies especially to mines, to a few fertile grain belts, to woods with good lumber, to salt works, and to important fisheries. Domination here, therefore, means permanent administration, by making the subjects work these for the ruling class. It is only later in the development, that there arises a taste for "lands and serfs" and large domains for the ruling class *beyond the confines of the narrow and original limits of the State.* This happens when the maritime state by the incorporation of subjugated territories has become a mixture of the territorial and the maritime forms. But even in that case, and in contradistinction to territorial states, large landed properties are merely a source of money rentals, and are in nearly all cases administered as absentee-property. This we find in Carthage and in the later Roman Empire.

The interests of the master class, which in the maritime state as well as in every other state, governs according to its own advantage, are different from those in the territorial state. In the latter the feudal territorial magnate is powerful because of his ownership of lands and people; while conversely, the patrician of the maritime city is powerful because of his wealth. The territorial magnate can dominate his "State" only by the number of men-at-arms maintained by him, and in order to have as many of these as possible, he must increase his territory as much as possible. The patrician, on the other hand, can control his "state" only by movable wealth, with which he can hire strong arms or bribe weak souls; such wealth is won faster by piracy, and by trade than by land wars and the possession of large estates in distant territories. Furthermore, in order thoroughly to use such property, he would be obliged to leave his city to settle down on it, and to become a regular squire; because in a period when money has not yet become general, where a profitable division of labor between town and country has not yet come about, the exploitation of large estates can only be carried on by actually consuming their products, and absentee ownership as a source of income is inconceivable. Thus far, however, we have not reached that portion of the development. We are still examining primitive conditions. No patrician of any city state would, at this time, think of leaving his lively rich home, in order to bury himself among barbarians, and thus with one move cut himself off in his state from any political rôle. All his economic, social and political interests impel him with one accord toward maritime ventures. Not landed property, but movable capital, is the sinew of his life.

These were the moving causes of the actions of the master class in the maritime cities; and even where geographical conditions permitted an extensive expansion beyond the adjoining *hinterland* of these cities, they turned the weight of effort toward sea-power rather than toward territorial growth. Even in the case of Carthage, its colossal territory was of far less importance to it than its maritime interests. Primarily it conquered Sicily and Corsica more in order to check the competition of the Greek and Etruscan traders than for the sake of owning these islands; it extended its territories toward the Lybians largely to insure the security of its other home possessions; and finally, when it conquered Spain, its ultimate reason was the need of owning the mines. The history of the *Hansa* shows many points of similarity to the above. The majority of these maritime cities, moreover, were not capable of subjugating a large district. Even had there been the will to conquer, there were extraneous, geographical conditions that hindered. All along the Mediterranean, with the exception of some few places, the coastal plain is extremely narrow, a small strip fenced off by high mountain ranges. That was one cause which prevented most of the states grouped about some trading harbor from growing to anything like the size we should naturally assume to be probable; while in the open country, ruled by herdsmen, and this very early, immense realms came into being. The second cause for the small beginnings of these states is found in this, that the *hinterland* whether in the hills or on the few plains of the Mediterranean was occupied by warlike tribes. These tribesmen, either hunters or warlike herdsmen, or else primitive feudal states of the same master race as the sea nomads, were not likely to be subjugated without a severe contest. Thus in Greece the interior was saved from the maritime states.

For these reasons the maritime State, even when most developed, always remains centralized, one is tempted to say centered, on its trading harbor; while the territorial State, strongly decentralized from the start, for a long time continues to develop as it expands a still more pronounced decentralization. Later, we shall see how this is affected by the adoption of those forms of government and of economic achievement which first were perfected in the "city-state," and which thus obtained the strength to counteract the centrifugal forces, and to build up the central organization which is characteristic of our modern states. This is the first great contrast between the two forms of the State.

No less decisive is the second point of contrast, whereby the territorial State remains tied up to natural economies as opposed to money economies, toward which the maritime State quickly turns. This contrast grows also out of the basic conditions of their existence.

Wherever a State lives in natural economy, money is a superfluous luxury—so superfluous that an economy developed to the use of money retrogrades again into a system of payments in kind as soon as the community drops back into the primitive form. Thus after Charlemagne had issued good coins, the economic situation expelled them. Neustria—not to mention Austrasia—under the stress of the migration of the peoples reverted to payment in kind. Such a system can well do without money as a standard of values, since it is without any developed intercourse and traffic. The lord's tenants furnish as tribute those things that the lord and his followers consume immediately; while his ornaments, fine fabrics, damascened arms, or rare horses, salt, etc., are procured in exchange with wandering merchants for slaves, wax, furs and other products of a warlike economic system of exchange in kind.

In city life, at any advanced stage of development, it is impossible to exist without a common measure of values. The free mechanic in a city can not, except in rare cases, find some other craftsman in need of the special thing which he produces, prepared to consume it immediately. Then, too, in cities the inevitable retail trade in food products, where every one must purchase nearly everything required, makes the use of coined money quite inevitable. It is impossible to conduct trade in its more limited sense, not between merchant and customers, but between merchant and merchant, without having a common measure of value. Imagine the case of a trader entering a port with a cargo of slaves, wishing to take cloth as a return cargo, and finding a cloth merchant who at the time may not want slaves but iron, or cattle, or furs. To accomplish this exchange, at least a dozen intermediate trades would have to take place before the object could be achieved. That can be avoided only if there exists some one commodity desired by all. In the system of payment in kind of the territorial states this may be taken by cattle or horses, since they may be used by any one at some time; but the ship owner can not load with cattle as a means of payment, and thus gold and silver become recognized as "money."

From centralization and from the use of money, which are the necessary properties of

the maritime or the *city State,* as we shall hereafter call it, its fate follows of necessity.

The psychology of the townsman, and especially of the dweller in the maritime commercial city, is radically different from that
of the countryman. His point of view is freer
and more inclusive, even though it be more
superficial; he is livelier, because more impres-
sions strike him in a day than a peasant in a
year. He becomes used to constant changes
and news, and thus is always *novarum rerum
cupidus.* He is more remote from nature and
less dependent on it than is the peasant, and
therefore he has less fear of "ghosts." One
consequence of this is that an underling in a
city State is less apt to regard the "taboo" regulations imposed on him by the first and second
estates of rulers. And as he is compelled to
live in compact masses with his fellow subjects,
he early finds his strength in numbers, so that
he becomes more unruly and seditious than the
serf who lives in such isolation that he never
becomes conscious of the mass to which he belongs and ever remains under the impression

that his overlord with his followers would have the upper hand in every fight.

This in itself brings about an ever progressive dissolution of the rigid system of subordinated groups first created by the feudal state. In Greece the territorial states alone were able to keep their subjects for a long time in a state of subjection: Sparta its Helots, Thessaly its *Penestæ*. In all the city States, on the other hand, we early find an uprising of the proletariat against which the master class was unable to oppose an effective resistance.

The economic situation tends toward the same result as the conditions of settlement. Movable wealth had far less stability than landed property: the sea is tricky, and the fortunes of maritime war and piracy not less so. The rich man of to-day may lose all by a turn of Fortune's wheel; while the poorest man may, by the same swing, land on top. But in a commonwealth based entirely on possessions, loss of fortune brings with it loss of rank and of "class," just as the converse takes place. The rich Plebeian becomes the leader of the

mass of the people in their constitutional fight
for equal rights and places all his fortune at
risk in that struggle. The position of the patricians becomes untenable; when coerced they
have ever conceded the claims of the lower
class. As soon as the first rich Plebeian has
been taken into their ranks, the right of rule
by birth, defended as a holy institution, has for-
ever become impossible. ' Henceforth it follows that what is fair for one is fair for the
other; and the aristocratic rule is followed first
by the plutocratic, then by the democratic,
finally by the ochlocratic régime, until either
foreign conquest or the "tyranny" of some *mob rule*
"Savior of the Sword" rescues the community
from chaos.

This end affects not only the State, but in
most cases its inhabitants so profoundly that
one may speak of a literal *death of the peoples,*
caused by the *capitalistic exploitation of slave
labor.* This latter is a social institution inevitably bound to exist in every state founded on
piracy and maritime ventures and thus coming
to use money as a means of exchange. In the

primitive stages of feudalism, whence it was derived, slavery was harmless, as is true in all economic systems based on exchange and use in kind, only to become an ulcerating cancer, utterly destructive of the entire life of the State as soon as it is exploited by the "capitalist" method, i. e., as soon as slave labor is applied, not to be used in a system of a feudal payment in kind, but to supply a market paying in money.

- Numberless slaves are brought into the country by piracy, privateering, or by the commercial wars. The wealth of their owners permits them to work the ground more intensively, and the owners of realty within the confines of the city limits draw ever increasing revenues from their possessions, and become more and more greedy of land. The small freeholder in the country, overburdened by the taxes and military service of wars waged in the interests of this great merchant class, sinks into debt, becomes a slave for debt, or migrates into the city as a pauper. But even so there is no hope for him, since the removal of the peasants has damaged the craftsmen and small traders, for the peasants were wont to purchase in the city, while the great estates, constantly increasing by the removal of the peasantry, supply their own needs by their own slave products. The evil attacks other parts of the body politic. The remaining trades are gradually usurped by masters exploiting slave labor, which is cheaper than free labor. The middle class thus goes to pieces; and a pauper, good-for-nothing mob, a genuine "bob-tail proletariat" comes into being, which, by reason of the democratic constituton achieved in the interim, is the sovereign of the commonwealth. The full course, political as well as military, is then a mere question of time. It may take place without a foreign invasion; which, however, usually sets in, when by reason of the physical breakdown caused by the immense depopulation, by the consumption of the people in its literal sense, the final stage is attained. This is the end of all these states. Within the scope of this treatise we can not dilate on this phase.

Only one city State was able to maintain it-

self throughout the centuries, because it was
the ultimate conqueror of all the others, and
because it was enabled to counteract the consumption of population by the only method of
sanitation possible; by extensive recreations of
middle class populations, both in cities and in
country districts, as well as by vast colonizations of peasants on lands taken from the
vanquished.

The Roman Empire was that state. But
even this gigantic organism finally succumbed
to the consumption of population, caused by
capitalistic slave exploitation. In the interval,
however, it had created the first *imperium,* i. e.,
the first tensely centralized state on a large
scale, and had overcome and amalgamated all
territorial states of both the Mediterranean
shores and its neighboring countries, and had
thereby for all time set before the world the
model of such an organized dominion. In addition to this it had developed the organization
of cities and of the system of money economy
to such an extent that they never were utterly
destroyed, even in the turmoil of the barbarian

migration.   In consequence of this, the feudal territorial states that occupied the territory of the former Roman Empire either directly or indirectly received those new impulses which were to carry them beyond the condition of the normal primitive feudal State.

CHAPTER V

THE DEVELOPMENT OF THE FEUDAL STATE

(a) THE GENESIS OF LANDED PROPERTY

WE now return, as stated above, to that point where the primitive feudal State gave rise to the city State as an offshoot, to follow the upward growth of the main branch. As the destiny of the city State was determined by the agglomeration of that form of wealth about which the State swung in its orbit, so the fate of the territorial State is conditioned by that agglomeration of wealth which in turn controls its orbit, the *ownership of landed property.*

In the preceding, we followed the economic differentiation in the case of the shepherd tribes, and showed that even here the law of the agglomeration about existing nuclei of wealth begins to assert its efficacy, as soon as the political means comes into play, be it in the form of wars for booty or still more in the form of slavery. We saw that the tribe had differentiated nobles and common freemen, beneath whom slaves, being without any political rights, are subordinated as a third class. This differentiation of wealth is introduced into the primitive state, and sharpens very markedly the contrast of social rank. It becomes still more accentuated by settlement, whereby private ownership in lands is created. Doubtless there existed even at the time when the primitive feudal state came into being, great differences in the amount of lands possessed by individuals, especially if within the tribe of herdsmen the separation had been strongly marked between the prince-like owners of large herds and many slaves, and the poorer common freemen. These princes occupy more land than do the small freemen.

At first, this happens quite harmlessly, and without a trace of any consciousness of the fact that extended possession of land will become the means of a considerable increase of social power and of wealth. Of this, there is at this time no question, since at this stage the common freemen would have been powerful enough to prevent the formation of extended landed estates had they known that it would eventually do them harm. But no one could have foreseen this possibility. Lands, in the condition in which we are observing them, have no value. For that reason the object and the spoils of the contest were not the possession of *lands,* but of *the land and its peasants, the latter being bound to the soil (glebæ adscripti* of our later law) as labor substrat and labor motors, from the conjunction of which there grows the object of the political means, viz., ground rent.

Every one is at liberty to take as much of *the uncultivated land* existing in masses as he needs and will or can cultivate. It is quite as unlikely that any one would care to measure off for another parts of an apparently limitless supply, as that any one would apportion the supply of atmospheric air.

The princes of the noble clans, probably from the start, pursuant to the usage of the tribe of herdsmen, receive more "lands and peasants" than do the common freemen. That is their right as princes, because of their position as patriarchs, war lords, and captains maintaining their warlike suites of half-free persons, of servants, of clients, or of refugees. This probably amounts to a considerable difference in the primitive amounts of land ownership. But this is not all. The princes need a larger surface of the *"land without peasants"* than do the common freemen, because they bring with them their servants and slaves. These have, however, no standing at law, and are incapable, according to the universal concepts of folk law, of acquiring title to landed property. Since, however, they must have land in order to live, their master takes it for them, so as to settle them thereon. In consequence of this, the richer the prince of the nomad tribe the more powerful the territorial magnate becomes.

But this means that wealth, and with it social rank, is consolidated more firmly and more durably than in the stage of herdsman ownership. For the greatest herds may be lost, but landed property is indestructible; and men bound to labor, bringing forth rentals, reproduce their kind even after the most terrible slaughter, even should they not be obtainable full grown in slave hunts.

About this fixed nucleus of wealth, property begins to agglomerate with increasing rapidity. Harmless as was the first occupation, men must soon recognize the fact that rental increases with the number of slaves one can settle on the unoccupied lands. Henceforth, the external policy of the feudal state is no longer directed toward the acquisition of land and peasants, but rather of peasants without land, to be carried off home as serfs, and there to be colonized anew. When the entire state carries on the war or the robbing expedition, the nobles obtain the lion's share. Very often, however, they go off on their own account, followed only by their suites, and then the common freeman, staying at home, receives no share in the loot. Thus the vicious circle constantly tends rapidly to enlarge with the increasing wealth of the

lands owned by the nobles.   The more slaves a
noble has, the more rental he can obtain.
With this, in turn, he can maintain a warlike
following, composed of servants, of lazy freemen, and of refugees.   With their help, he
can, in turn, drive in so many more slaves, to
increase his rentals.

This process takes place, even where some
central power exists, which, pursuant to the
general law of the people, has the right to dis-
pose of uncultivated lands; while it is, in many
cases, not only by sufferance, but often by the
express sanction of that authority.   As long as
the feudal magnate remains the submissive vassal of the crown, it lies in the king's interest to
make him as strong as possible.   By this means·
his military suite, to be placed at the disposal
of the crown in times of war, is correspond-
ingly increased.   We shall adduce only one il-
lustration to show that the necessary consequence in universal history is not confined to
the well-known effect in the feudal states of
Western Europe, but follows from these premises even under totally different surroundings:

"The principal service in Fiji consisted in war duty; and if the outcome was successful it meant new grants of lands, including therein the denizens, as slaves, and thus led to the assumption of new obligations." [91]

This accumulation of landed property in ever increasing quantity in the hands of the landed nobility brings the primitive feudal state of a higher stage to the "finished feudal state" with a complete scale of feudal ranks.

Reference to a previous work by the author, based on a study of the sources, will show the same causal connection for German lands; [92] and in that publication it was pointed out that in all the instances noted a process takes place, identical in its principal lines of development. It is only on this line of reasoning that one can explain the fact, to take Japan as an example, that its feudal system developed into the precise details which are well known to the students of European history, although Japan is inhabited by a race fundamentally different from the Arians; and besides (a strong argument against giving too great weight to the materialistic view of history) the process of agriculture is on a totally different technical basis, since the Japanese are not cultivators with the plow, but with the hoe.

In this instance, as throughout this book, it is not the fortune of a single people that is investigated; it is rather the object of the author to narrate the typical development, the universal consequences, of the same basic traits of mankind wherever they are placed. Presupposing a knowledge of the two most magnificent examples of the expanded feudal state, Western Europe and Japan, we shall, in general, limit ourselves to cases less well known, and so far as possible give the preference to material taken from ethnography, rather than from history in its more restricted sense.

The process now to be narrated is a change, gradually consummated but fundamentally revolutionary, of the political and social articulation of the primitive feudal state: *the central authority loses its political power to the territorial nobility, the common freeman sinks from his status, while the "subject" mounts.*

(b) THE CENTRAL POWER IN THE PRIMITIVE FEUDAL STATE

The patriarch of a tribe of herdsmen, though endowed with the authority which flows from his war-lordship and sacerdotal functions, generally has no despotic powers. The same may be said of the "king" of a small settled community, where, generally speaking, he would exercise very limited command. On the other hand, as soon as some military genius manages to fuse together numerous tribes of herdsmen into one powerful mass of warriors, despotic centralized power is the direct, inevitable consequence.[98] As soon as war exists, the truth of the Homeric

οὐκ ἀγαθὴ πολυκοιρανίη, εἷς κοίρανος ἔστω
εἷς βασιλεύς,*

is admitted by the most unruly tribes, and becomes a fact to be acted on. The free primitive huntsmen render to their elected chief unconditioned obedience, while on the war-path;

* "The rule of the many is not a good thing, over the many there should be one king."

the free Cossacks of the Ukraine, recognizing
no authority in times of peace, submit to their
hetman's power of life and death in times of
war. This obedience toward their war-lord is
a trait common to every genuine warrior
psychology.

The leaders of the great migrations of nomads are all powerful despots: Attila, Omar,
Genghis Khan, Tamerlane, Mosilikatse,
Ketchwayo. Similarly, we find that whenever
a mighty territorial state has come into being
as the result of the welding together of a number of primitive feudal states, there existed in
the beginning a strong central authority. Examples of this may be seen in the case of Sar-
gon Cyrus, Chlodowech, Charlemagne, Boleslaw the Red. Sometimes, especially as long
as the main state has not yet reached its geographical or sociologic bounds, the centralized
authority is maintained intact in the hands of a
series of strong monarchs, which degenerates,
in some instances, to the maddest despotism
and insanity of some of the Cæsars: especially
do we find flagrant examples of this in Meso-

potamia and in Africa. We shall merely
touch on this phase: the more so, as it has little
general effect on the final development of the
forms of government. This point should,
however, be stated, that the development of the
form of government of a despotism depends
in the main, on what the *sacerdotal* status of
the rulers may be, in addition to their position
as war-lords, and whether or not they hold the
monopoly of trade as an additional regalian
right.

The combination of Cæsar and Pope tends
in all cases to develop the extreme forms of despotism; while the partition of spiritual and
temporal functions brings it about that their
exponents mutually check and counterbalance
one another. A characteristic example may
be found in the conditions prevailing among
the Malay states of the East Indian Archipelago, genuine "maritime states," whose genesis
is an exact counterpart of that of the Greek
maritime states. Generally speaking, the
prince has just as little power among these, as,
shall we say, the king at the opening of the his-

tory of the Attic states. The chieftains of the
clans (in Sulu the Dato, in Achin the Panglima), as in the case of Athens, have the real
power. But where, "as in Tobah, religious
motives endow the rulers with the position of
a Pope in miniature, an entirely different
phase is found. The Panglima then depend
entirely on the Rajah, and are merely officials." [94] To refer to a well-known fact,
when the aristocrats and chiefs of the clans in
Athens and in Rome abolished the kingdom,
they preserved at least the old *title,* and
granted its use to a dignitary otherwise politically impotent, in order that the gods might
have their offerings presented in the accustomed manner. For the same reason, in many
cases, the descendant of the former tribal king
is preserved as a dignitary, otherwise totally
powerless, while the actual power of government has long since been transferred to some
war chief; as in the later Merovingian Empire,
the Carolingian Mayors of the palace (Majordomus) ruled alongside a "long locked king,"
rex crinitus, of the race of Merowech, so, in

Japan, the Shogun ruled beside the Mikado, and in the Empire of the Incas, the commander of the Inca beside the Huillcauma, who had been gradually limited to his sacerdotal functions.* [95]

In addition to the office of supreme pontiff, the power of the head of the state is frequently increased enormously by the trading monopoly, a function exercised by the primitive chieftains as a natural consequence of the peaceful barter of guest-gifts. Such a trade monopoly, for example, was exercised by King Solomon; and latterly by the Roman Emperor Friedrich II.† [96]

As a rule, the negro chieftains are "monopolists of trading"; [97] as is the King of Sulu. [98] Among the Galla, wherever the supremacy of a head chief is acknowledged, he becomes "as

---

* In Egypt we find a similar state of affairs, beside the bigoted Amenhotep IV., the Majordomus of the palace Haremheb, who "managed to unite in his hands the highest military and administrative functions of the empire, until he exercised the powers of a regent of the state." Schneider, *Civilization and Thought of the Ancient Egyptians.* Leipzig, 1907, page 22.

† Cf. *Acta Imperii*, or *Huillard-Breholles, H. D. Fred. II.* —*Translator.*

a matter of course, the tradesman for his tribe; since none of his subjects is allowed to trade with strangers directly." [99]   Among the Barotse and Mabunda, the king is "according to the strict interpretation of the law, the only trader of his country." [100]

Ratzel notes, in telling language, the importance of this factor: "In addition to his witchcraft, the chief increases his power by a *monopoly of trading*. Since the chief is the sole intermediary in trade, everything desired by his subjects passes through his hands, and he becomes the donor of all longed-for gifts, the fulfiller of the fondest wishes. In such a system, there lie certainly the possibilities of great power." [101]   If, in conquered districts, where the power of government is apt to be more tensely exercised, there is added the monopoly of trade, the royal power may become very great.

It may be stated as a general rule, that even in the apparently most extreme cases of *despotism,* no monarchical *absolutism* exists. The ruler may, undeterred by fear of punishment,

rage against his subject class; but he is checked
in no small degree by his feudal followers.
Ratzel, in speaking of the subject generally,
remarks: "The so-called 'court assemblage'
of African or of ancient American chiefs is
probably always a council. . . . Although we
meet with traces of absolutism with all peoples
on a low scale, even where the form of government is republican, the cause of absolutism is
not in the strength of either the state or of the
chieftain, but in the moral weakness of the individual, who succumbs without any effective
resistance to the powers wielded over him." [102]
The kingdom of the Zulu is a limited despotism, in which very powerful ministers of state
(Induna) share the power; with other Caffir
tribes it is a council, sometimes dominating
both people and chieftains.[103]   In spite of this
control "under Tshaka every sneezing or
hawking in the presence of the tyrant, as well
as every lack of tears at the death of some royal
kinsman, was punished with death." [104]   The
same limitation applies to the West African
kingdoms of Dahomy and Ashanti, notorious

because of their frightful barbarities. "In spite of the waste of human life, in war, slave trade, and human sacrifices, there existed at no place absolute despotism. . . . Bowditch remarks on the similarity of the system prevailing in Ashanti, with its ranks and orders, with the old Persian system as described by Herodotus." [105]

One must be very careful, and this may again be insisted upon, not to confuse despotism with absolutism. Even in the feudal states of Western Europe, the rulers exercised, in many cases, power of life and death, free from the trammels of law; but nevertheless such a ruler was impotent as against his "magnates." So long as he does not interfere with the privileges of the classes, he need not restrain his cruelty, and he may even occasionally sacrifice one of the great men; but woe to him were he to dare to touch the economic privileges of his magnates. It is possible to study this very characteristic phase, completely free, from the standpoint of law, and yet closely hemmed in by political checks, in the great East African empires: "The government of Waganda and Wanyoro is, in theory, based on the rule of the king over the whole territory; but in reality this is only the semblance of government, since, as a matter of fact, the lands belong to the supreme chieftains of the empire. It was they who represented the popular opposition to foreign influences, in the time of Mtesa; and Muanga did not dare, for fear of them, to carry out any innovations. Although the kingship is limited in reality, yet in form it occupies an imposing position in unessentials. The ruler is absolute master over the lives and limbs of his subjects, the mass of the people, and feels himself restrained only in the narrowest circle of the chief courtiers." [106]

Precisely the same statement applies to the inhabitants of Oceania, to mention the last of the great societies that created states: "At no place does one find an entire absence of a representative mediation between prince and people. . . . The aristocratic principle corrects the patriarchal. Therefore, the extremes of *despotism* depend more on class and caste pressure than on the overpowering will of any individual." [107]

(c) THE POLITICAL AND SOCIAL DISINTEGRATION OF THE PRIMITIVE FEUDAL STATE

Space forbids our detailing the innumerable shadings under which the patriarchal-aristocratic (in some cases plutocratic) mixture of form of government in the primitive feudal state is shown in either an ethnographic, historical or juristic survey. This is likewise of the greatest importance for the subsequent development.

It is indifferent how much power the ruler may have had at the beginning, an inevitable fate breaks down his power in a short while; and does this, one may say, the faster, the greater that power was, i. e., the larger the territory of the primitive feudal state of higher grade.

Taking into account the process already set forth, which, through the occupation and settlement of unused lands by means of newly acquired slaves, made for the increase of power

of the separate nobles, a result came about
which might prove uncomfortable for the central power. Mommsen in speaking of the
Celts says: "When in a clan numbering about
eighty thousand armed men, a single chieftain
could appear at convocation with ten thousand
followers, exclusive of his serfs and debtors, it
becomes clear that such a noble was rather an
independent prince than a mere citizen of his
clan." [108] And the same may apply to the
"Heiu" of the Somali, where a great landed
proprietor maintained hundreds of families in
dependence on his lands, "so that conditions
in Somaliland tend to recall those existing
in mediæval Europe during feudal times." [109]

Although such a preponderance of isolated
territorial magnates can come about in the feudal state of low development, it nevertheless
reaches its culmination in the feudal state of
higher grade, the great feudal state; this happens by reason of the increased power given
to the landlords by the bestowal of *public official functions.*

The more the state expands, the more must

official power be delegated by the central government to its representatives on the borders
and marches, who are constantly threatened by
wars and insurrectionary outbreaks. In order
to preserve his bailiwick in safety for the state,
such an official must be endowed with supreme
military powers, joined with the functions of
the highest administrative officials. Even
should he not require a large number of civil
employees, he still must have a permanent military force. And how is he to pay these men?
With one possible exception, to be noted hereafter, there are no taxes which flow into the
treasury of the central government and then
are poured back again over the land, since
these presuppose an economic development
existing only where money is employed. But
in communities having a system of payments
in kind, such as these "territorial states" all are,
there are no taxes payable in money. For that
reason, the central government has no alter-
native but to turn over to the counts, or border
wardens, or satraps, the income of its territorial jurisdiction. Such an official, then, re-

ceives the dues of the subjects, determines when and where forced labor is to be rendered, receives the deodands, fees and penalties payable in cattle, etc.; and in consideration of these must maintain the armed force, place definite numbers of armed men at the disposal of the central government, build and maintain highways and bridges, feed and stable the ruler and his following, or his "royal messengers," and finally, furnish a definite "Sergeantry" consisting of highly valuable goods, easily transported to the court, such as horses, cattle, slaves, precious metals, wines, etc.

In other words, he receives an immensely large fief for his services. If previously he was not, he now becomes the greatest man in his country, though before he probably was the most powerful landlord in his official district. He will hereafter do exactly what his equals in rank are doing, although they may not have his official position; that is to say, he will, only on a larger scale, continue to settle new lands with ever newly recruited serfs. By this he increases his military strength; and this must

be wished for and aided by the central government. For it is the fate of these states, that
they must fatten those very local powers, that
are to engulf them.

Conditions arise which enable the warden
of the marches to impose the terms of his military assistance, especially in the inevitable
feuds which arise over the right of succession
to the central government. Thereby he obtains further valuable concessions, especially
the formal acknowledgment of the heritability
of his official fief, so that office and lands come
to be held by an identical tenure. By this
means, he gradually becomes almost independent of the central authority, and the complaint
of the Russian peasant, "The sky is high up
and the Tsar is far off," tends to become of universal application. Take this characteristic example from Africa: "The empire of Lunda is
an absolute feudal state. The chieftains (Muata, Mona, Muene) are permitted independent
action in all internal affairs, so long as it
pleases the Muata Jamvo. Usually, the great
chieftains, living afar, send their caravans with

their tribute once a year to the Mussumba; but *those living at too great a distance, sometimes for long periods omit making any payments of their tribute;* while similar chiefs in the neighborhood of the capital forward tribute many times a year." [110]

Nothing can show more plainly than this report, how, because of inadequate means of transportation, extent of distance becomes politically effective in these states loosely held together and in a state of payment in kind. One is tempted to say that the independence of the feudal masters grows in proportion to the square of their distance from the seat of the central authority. The crown must pay more and more for their services, and must gradually confirm them in all the sovereign powers of the state, or else permit their usurpation of these powers after they have seized them one after the other. Such are heritability of fiefs, tolls on highways and commerce, (in a later stage the right of coinage), high and low justice, the right to exact for private gain the public duties of repair of ways and bridges (the old

English *trinodis necessitas*) and the disposal of the military services of the freemen of the country.

By these means, the powerful frontier wardens gradually attain an ever greater, and finally a complete, *de facto* independence, even though the *formal* bond of feudal suzerainty may for a long time apparently keep together the newly developed principalities. The reader, of course, recalls instances of these typical transitions; all mediæval history is one chain of them; not only the Merovingian and Carolingian Empires, not only Germany, but also France, Italy, Spain, Poland, Bohemia, Hungary, as well as Japan and China,[111] have passed through this process of decomposition, not only once, but repeatedly. And this is no less true of the feudal states of Mesopotamia: great empires follow each other, acquire power, burst asunder time after time, and again are re-united. In the case of Persia, we are expressly told: "Separate states and provinces, by a successful revolt, obtained freedom for a longer or shorter time, and the 'great king'

at Susa did not always have the power to
force them to return to their obedience; in
other states, the satraps or warlike chieftains
ruled arbitrarily, carrying on the government
faithlessly and violently, either as independent
rulers or tributary under-kings of the king of
kings.   The Persian world-empire went to its
disintegration an agglomeration of states and
lands, without any general law, without ordered administration, without uniform judicial
system, without order and enforcement of law,
and without possibility of help." [112]

A similar fate overtook its neighbor in the
valley of the Nile: "Princes spring from
the families of the usurpers, free landlords, who
pay land-taxes to nobody but to the king, and
rule over certain strips of land, or districts.
These district princes govern a territory specifically set apart as pertaining to their official
position, and separate from their family possessions.

"Later successful warlike operations, perhaps filling in the gap between the Ancient and
the Middle (Egyptian) Empire, *together with*

the gathering in of captives of the wars, who could be utilized as labor motors, brought a more stringent exploitation of the subjects, a definite determination of the tributes. During the Middle Empire, the power of the princes of the clans rose to an enormous height, they maintained great courts, imitating the splendor of the royal establishment." [113] "With the decline of the royal authority during a period of decay, the higher officials use their power for personal aims, in order to make their offices hereditary within their families." * [114]

But the operation of this historical law is

* Maspero says, *New Light on Ancient Egypt,* pp. 218-9: "Until then, in fact, the high priest had been chosen and nominated by the king; from the time of Rameses III. he was always chosen from the same family, and the son succeeded his father on the pontifical throne. From that time events marched quickly. The Theban mortmain was doubled with a veritable seigniorial fief, which its masters increased by marriages with the heirs of neighboring fiefs, by continual bequests from one branch of the family to the other, and by *the placing of cadets of each generation at the head of the clergy of certain secondary towns.* The official protocol of the offices filled by their wives shows that a century or a century and a half after Rameses III., almost the whole of the Thebaid, about a third of the Egyptian territory was in the hands of the High Priest of Ammon and of his family."—*Translator's Note (and italics).*

not restricted to the "historical" peoples. In
speaking of the feudal states of India, Ratzel
states: "Even beyond Radshistan, the nobles
often enjoyed a great measure of independence, so that even in Haiderabad, after the
Nizam had acquired the sole rule over the
country, the Umara or Nabobs maintained
troops of their own, independently of the army
of the Nizam. These smaller feudatories did
not comply with the increased demands of
modern times as regards the administration of
Indian states as often as did the greater
princes." [115]

In Africa finally, great feudal states come
and pass away, as do bubbles arising and burst-
ing from the stream of eternally similar
phenomena. The powerful Ashanti empire,
within one and a half centuries, has shriveled
to less than one-fifth of its territory; [116] and
many of the empires that the Portuguese en-
countered have since disappeared without
leaving a trace of their existence. And yet
these were strong feudal powers: "Stately
and cruel negro empires, such as Benin,

Dahomy or Ashanti, resemble in many respects ancient Peru or Mexico, having in their vicinity politically disorganized tribes. The hereditary nobility of the Mfumus, sharply separated from the rest of the state, had mainly the administration of the districts, and together with the more transitory nobility of service, formed in Loango strong pillars of the ruler and his house." [117]

But whenever such a state, once powerful, has split into a number of territorial states either *de facto* or juristically independent, the former process begins anew. The great state gobbles up the smaller ones, until a new empire has arisen. "The greatest territorial magnates later become emperors," says Meitzen laconically of Germany.[118] But even this great demesne vanishes, split up by the need of equipping warlike vassals with fiefs. "The Kings soon found that they had donated away all their belongings; their great territorial possessions in the Delta had melted away," says Schneider (l. c. page 38) of the Pharaohs of the sixth dynasty. The same causes brought about like effects in the Frankish Empire among both Merovingians and Carolingians; and later in Germany in the case of the Saxon and Hohenstaufen Emperors.[119] Additional references are unnecessary, as every one is familiar with these instances.

In a subsequent part of this treatise, we shall examine into the causes that finally liberated the primitive feudal state from this witch's curse, this circling from agglomeration to disintegration without end. Our present task is to take up the *social* side of the process, as we have already taken up the historical phase of it. It changes the articulation of classes in the most decisive manner.

The common freemen, the lower strata of the dominating group, are struck with overpowering force. They sink into bondsmenship. Their decay must go along with that of the central power; since both, allied one might say, by nature, are menaced simultaneously by the expanding power of the great territorial lords. The crown controls the landed magnate so long as the levy of the common freemen of the district is a superior force to his guards, to his "following." But a fatal need, already set forth, impels the crown to deliver over the peasants to the landed lordling, and from the moment when the county levy has become weaker than his guards, the free peasants are lost. Where the sovereign powers of the state are delegated to the territorial magnate, i. e., where he has developed more or less into an independent lord of the region, the overthrow of the liberties of the peasants is carried out, at least in part, under the color of law, by forcing excessive military services, which ruin the peasants, and which are required the more often as the dynastic interests of the territorial lord require new lands and new peasants, or by abusing the right to compulsory labor, or by turning the administration of public justice into military oppression.

The common freemen, however, receive the final blow either by the formal delegation or by the usurpation of the most important powers of the crown, the disposition of unoccupied lands or "commons." Originally, this land be-

longed to all the "folk" in common; i. e., to the
freemen for common use; but in accordance
with an original custom, probably universal,
the patriarch enjoys disposal of it.   This right
of disposition passes to the territorial
magnate with the remaining royal privileges—and thus he has obtained the power
to strangle any few remaining freemen.   He
now declares all unoccupied lands his property,
and forbids their settlement by free peasants,
while those only are permitted access who
recognize his superior lordship; i. e., who have
commended themselves to him, or are his serfs.

That is the last nail in the coffin of the common freemen.   Heretofore their equality of
possessions has been in some way guaranteed.
Even if a peasant had twelve sons, his patri-
mony was not split up, because eleven of them
broke new hides of land in the commons of
the community, or else in the general land not
yet distributed to other villages.   That is
henceforth impossible; hides tend to divide
where large families grow up, others are
united when heir and heiress marry: hence-

forth there come into existence "laborers," recruited from the owners of half, a quarter, or even an eighth of a hide who help work a larger area. Thus the free peasantry splits into rich and poor; this begins to loosen the bond which hitherto had made the bundle of arrows unbreakable. When, therefore, some comrade is overwhelmed by the exactions of the lord and has become his liegeman, or if bond peasants are settled among the original owners, either to occupy some hide vacated by the extinction of the family or fallen into the hands of the lord because of the indebtedness of its occupant, then every social cohesion is loosened; and the peasantry, split apart by class and by economic contrasts, is handed over without power of resistance to the magnate.

On the other hand, the result is the same where the magnate has no usurped regalian powers of the state. In such cases, open force and shameless violation of rights accomplish the same ends. The ruler, far off and impotent, bound to rely on the good will and help of the violators of law and order, has

neither the power nor the opportunity of interference.

There is hardly any need of adducing instances. The free peasantry of Germany were
put through the process of expropriation and
declassification at least three times. Once it
happened in Celtic times.[120] The second overthrow of the free peasants of the old German
Empire took place in the ninth and tenth
centuries. The third tragedy of the same form
began with the fifteenth century, in the countries formerly Slavic, which they had conquered
and colonized.[121] The peasants fared worse
in those lands, in the "republics of nobles,"
where there was no monarchical central authority, whose community of interests with
their subjects tended to deprive oppression of
its worse features. The Celts in the Gaul of
Cæsar's time are one of the earliest examples.
Here "the great families exercised an economic, military and political preponderance.
They monopolized the leases of the lucrative
rights of the state. They forced the common
freemen, overwhelmed by the taxes which they

had themselves imposed, to borrow of them, and then, first as their debtors, afterward legally as their serfs, to surrender their liberty. For their own advantage they developed the system of followers: i. e., the privilege of the nobility to have about them a mass of armed servants in their pay, called *ambacti,* with whose aid they formed a state within a state. Relying on these, their own men-at-arms, they defied the lawful authorities and the levies of the freemen, and thus were able to burst asunder the commonwealth. . . . The only protection to be found was in the relation of serfdom, where personal duty and interest required the lord to protect his clients and to avenge any wrong to his men. Since the state no longer had the power to protect the freemen, these in growing numbers became the vassals of some powerful noble." [122] We find these identical conditions fifteen hundred years later in Kurland, Livonia, in Swedish Pomerania, in Eastern Holstein, in Mecklenburg, and especially in Poland. In the German territories the petty nobles subjugated their peasantry, while in Poland their prey was the formerly free and noble Schlachziz. "Universal history is monotonous," says Ratzel. The same procedure overthrew the peasantry of ancient Egypt: "After a warlike *intermezzo*, there follows a period in the history of the Middle Empire, which brings about a deterioration of the position of the peasantry in Lower Egypt. The number of landlords decreases, while their territorial growth and power increases. The tribute of the peasants is hereafter determined by an exact assessment on their estates, and definitely fixed by a sort of Doomsday Book. Because of this pressure, many peasants soon enter the lord's court or the cities of the local rulers, and take employment there either as servants, mechanics, or even as overseers in the economic organization of these manors or courts. In common with any available captives, they contribute to the extension of the prince's estates, and to further the general expulsion of the peasantry from their holdings." [128]

The example of the Roman Empire shows,

as nothing else can, how inevitable this process becomes.   When we first meet Rome in history the conception of serfdom or bondage has already been forgotten.   When the "modern period" of Rome opens, only slavery is known. And yet, within fifteen centuries, the free peasantry again sink into economic dependence, after Rome has become an overextended, unwieldy empire, whose border districts have more and more dissolved from the central control.   The great landed proprietors, having been endowed with the lower justice and police administration on their own estates have "reduced their servants, who may originally have been free proprietors of the *'ager privatus vectigalis'* to a state of servitude, and have thus developed a sort of actual *glebæ adscriptus,* within the boundaries of their 'immunities.' " [124]   The invading Germans found this feudal order worked out in Gaul and the other provinces.   At this particular time, the immense difference formerly existing between slaves and free settlers (*coloni*) had been completely obliterated, first in their economic position, and then, naturally, in their constitutional rights.

Wherever the common freemen sink into political and economic dependence on the great territorial magnates, when, in other words, they become bound either to the court or to the lands, the social group formerly subject to them tend in a corresponding measure to improve their status. Both layers tend to meet half-way, to approximate their position, and finally to amalgamate. The observations just made concerning the free settlers and the agricultural slaves of the later Roman Empire hold true everywhere. Thus in Germany, freemen and serfs together formed, when fused, the economic and legally unital group of *Grundholde,* or men bound to the soil.[125]

The elevation of the former "subjects," hereafter for the sake of brevity to be called "plebs," flows from the same source as the debasement of the freeman, and arises by the same necessity from the very foundations on which these states are themselves erected, viz., the agglomeration of the landed property in ever fewer hands.

The plebs are the natural opponents of the central government—since that is their conqueror and tax imposer; while they naturally oppose the common freemen, who despise them and oppress them politically, besides crowding them back economically. The great magnate also is the natural opponent of the central government—an impediment in his path toward complete independence, and he is at the same time also a natural enemy of the common freemen, who in turn not only support the central government; but also block with their possessions his path toward territorial dominion, while with their claims to equality of political rights they annoy his princely pride. Since the political and social interests of the territorial princes and of the plebs coincide, they must become allies; the prince can attain complete independence only if, in his fight for power against the crown and the common freemen, he controls reliable warriors and acquiescent taxpayers; the plebs can only then be freed from their pariah-like declassification, both economically and socially, if the hated and proud common freemen are brought down to their level.

This is the second time that we have noted the identity of interest between the princes and their subjects. The first time we found a weakly developed solidarity in our second stage of state formation. This causes the semi-sovereign prince to treat his dependent tenants as kindly as he ill-treats the free peasants of his territory; in consequence, they will fight the more willingly for him and contribute taxes, while the more readily will the oppressed freemen succumb to the pressure, especially as their share of political power in the state, coincident with the decline of the central power, has become only a meaningless phrase. In some cases, as in Germany toward the end of the tenth century, this was done with full consciousness of its effects [126]—some prince exercises a particularly "mild" rule, in order to draw the subjects of a neighboring potentate into his lands, and thus to increase his own:

strength in war and taxation, and to weaken his opponent's. The plebs come to possess, both legally and actually, constantly increasing rights, enlarged privileges of the law of ownership, perhaps self-government in common affairs, and their own administration of justice; thus they rise in the same degree as the common freemen sink, until the two classes meet and they are amalgamated into one body on approximately the same jural and economic plane. Half serfs, half subjects of a state, they represent a characteristic formation of the feudal state, which does not as yet recognize any clear distinction between public and private law; in its turn an immediate consequence of its own historical genesis, *the dominion in the form of a state for the sake of economic private rights.*

(d) THE ETHNIC AMALGAMATION

The juristic and social amalgamation of the degraded freemen and the uplifted plebs henceforth inevitably tends toward ethnic interpenetration. While at first the subject peoples were not allowed either to intermarry or to have social intercourse with the freemen, now no such obstacles can be maintained; in any single village the social class is no longer determined by descent from the ruling race, but rather by wealth. And the case may frequently arise where the pure-blooded descendant of the warrior herdsman must earn his living as a field hand in the hire of the equally pure-blooded descendant of the former serfs. The social group of the subjects is now composed of a part of the former ethnic master group and a part of the former subject group.

We say from a part only, because the other part has by this time been amalgamated with the other part of the old ethnic master group into a unital social class. In other words, a part of the plebs has not only attained the position to which the mass of the common freemen have sunk, but has climbed far beyond it, in that it has been completely received into the dominating group, which in the meantime, has not only risen enormously, but has been as greatly diminished in numbers.

And that, too, is a universal process found
in all history; because everywhere it follows
with equally compelling force from the very
premises of feudal dominion. The *primus
inter pares,* whether the holder of the central
power or some local potentate, taking the rank
of a prince, requires more supple tools for his
dominion than are to be found among his
"peers." The latter represent a class whom
he must put down if he wants to rise—and that
is and must be the aim of every one, since in
this stage aiming for power is identical with
the aim of self-preservation. In this effort he
is opposed by his obnoxious and stiff-necked
cousins and by his petty nobles—and for this
reason, we find at every court, from that of the
sovereign king of a mighty feudal empire down
to the lord of what is hardly more than a big
estate, men of insignificant descent as con-
fidential officials alongside representatives of
the master group, who in many cases under
the mask of officials of the prince, as a matter
of fact, are "ephors," sharers of the power of
the prince as the plenipotentiaries of their

group. Let us but recall the Induna at the court of the Bantu kings. There is no wonder, then, that the prince rather places confidence in his own men than in these annoying and pretentious advisers, in men whose position is indissolubly bound up with his own, and who would be ruined by his fall.*

Here, too, historical references are nearly superfluous. Every one is familiar with the fact that at the courts of the western European feudal kingdoms, besides the relatives of the king and some noble vassals, there were also elements from the lower groups, occupying high positions, clerics and great warriors of the plebeian class. Among the immediate following of Charlemagne all the races and peoples of his empire were represented. Also in the tales of Theodoric the Goth in the Dietrich Saga of the *Niebelungen Lied,* this

* One of the most notable instances may be found in the case of Markward of Annweiler, Marquis of Ancona and Duke of Ravenna, seneschal of Henry VI., who after the death of the Emperor Henry VI. disputed the power of the Regent Constance acting for her son, Frederick II. (See Boehmer-Ficker, *Regesta Imperii*, V, vol. 1, No. 511. v. ad. annum 1197.)—*Translator.*

rise of brave sons of the subject races finds
its reflection. In addition to these, there follow some less well-known instances.

In Egypt, as far back as the Old Empire,
there is found alongside the royal officials of
the feudal nobility, who are the descendants of
the Shepherd conquerors, administering their
districts as representatives of the crown, with
plenary powers as deputies, *"a mass of court
officials* trusted with determined functions of
government." It "originated with the *servants* employed at the courts of the princes,
such as prisoners of war, refugees etc." [127]
The fable of Joseph shows a state of affairs
known at that time to be a usual occurrence, of
the rise of a slave to the position of an all
powerful minister of state. At the present
day such a career is within the realm of possibility at any oriental court, such as Persia,
Turkey, or Morocco, etc. In the case of old
Marshal Derflinger, in the time of Friedrich
Wilhelm I., the Great Elector, at a much
later date, we have an example from the transition of the developed feudal state to a more

modern form of the state, which might be multiplied by the examples of innumerable other brave swordsmen.

Let us add a few instances from the peoples "disregarded by history." Ratzel tells of the realm of Bornu: "The freemen have not lost the consciousness of their free descent, in contrast with the slaves of the sheik; but the rulers place more confidence in their slaves than in their own kinsmen and free associates of their tribe. They can count on the devotion of the former. Not only positions at court, but the defense of the country was from ancient times preferably confided to slaves. The brothers of the prince, as well as the more ambitious or more efficient sons, are objects of suspicion; and while the most important places at court are in the hands of slaves, the princes are put at posts far from the seat of government. Their salaries are paid from the incomes of the offices and the taxes from the provinces." [128]

Among the Fulbe "society is divided into princes, chieftains, commons and slaves. The slaves of the king play a great rôle as soldiers and officials, and may hope for the highest offices in the state."[129]

This nobility of the court's creation may, in certain cases, be admitted to the great imperial offices, so that according to the method stated above, it may achieve the sovereignty over a territory. In the developed feudal state, it represents the high nobility; and usually manages to preserve its rank, even when some more powerful neighbor has mediatized it by incorporating the state. The Frankish higher nobility certainly contains such elements from the original lower group;[130] and since from its blood the entire upper nobility of the European civilized states has been descended at least in direct line by marriage, we find an ethnic amalgamation, both in the present day group of subjects and in the highest order of the ruling class. And the same applies to Egypt: "With the sinking of the royal authority in the time of the decay, the higher officials abuse their power for personal ends, to make their offices hereditary in their families, and thereby to call into existence an official nobility not differentiated from the rest of the population." [131]

And finally, the same process, from the same causes, takes hold of the present middle class, the lower stratum of the master class, the officials and officers of the great feudatories. At first there still exists a social difference between, on the one hand, the free vassals, the subfeudatories of the great landlord, kinsmen, younger sons of other noble families, impoverished associates from the same district, in isolated cases freeborn sons of peasants, free refugees and professional ruffians of free descent; and on the other, if the term may be allowed, the subalterns of the guards of plebeian descent. But lack of freedom advances, while freedom sinks in social value; and here too the ruler places more reliance on his creatures than on his peers. Here also, sooner or later, the process of amalgamation becomes complete. In Germany, as late as 1085, the non-free nobility of the court ranks between *"servi et litones"* while a century afterward it is placed with the *"liberi et nobiles."* In the course of the thirteenth century, it has been completely absorbed, along with the free vassals, into the nobility by chivalry. The two orders in the meantime tend to become equal economically; both have subinfeudations, fiefs on the obligation of service in warfare, and the service feuds of the bondsmen; while all the fiefs of the "ministerials" or sergeants have in the meantime become as heritable as are those of the free vassals, as much so as are the patrimonies of the few surviving smaller territorial lords belonging to the original nobility, who may still have escaped the grasp of the great territorial principalities.

In ways quite analogous to this the development went on in all other feudal states of Western Europe; while its exact counterpart is found in the extremest Orient on the edge of the Eurasian continent, in Japan. The daimio are the higher nobility; the samurai, the chivalry, the nobility of the sword.

(e) THE DEVELOPED FEUDAL STATE

With this the feudal state has reached its pinnacle. It forms, politically and socially, a hierarchy of numerous strata; of which, in all cases, the lower is bound to render service to the next above it, and the superior is bound to render protection to the one below. The pyramid rests on the laboring population, of whom the major part are as yet peasants; the surplus of their labor, the ground rental, the entire "surplus value" of the economic means is used to support the upper strata of society. This ground rent from the majority of estates is turned over to the small holders of fiefs, except where these estates are still in the immediate possession of the prince or of the crown and have not as yet been granted as fiefs. The holders of them are bound in return to provide the stipulated military service, and also, in certain cases, to render labor of an economic value. The larger vassal is in turn bound to serve the great tenants of the crown; who in their turn are, at least at strict law, under similar obligation toward the bearer of the central power; while emperor, king, sultan, shah, or Pharaoh in their turn, are regarded as the vassals of the tribal god. Thus there starts from the fields, whose peasantry support and nourish all, and mounts up to the "king of heaven" an artificially graded order of ranks, which constricts so absolutely all the life of the state, that according to custom and law neither a bit of land nor a man can be understood unless within its fold. Since all rights originally created for the common freemen have either been resumed by the state, or else have been distorted by the victorious princes of territories, it comes about that a person not in some feudal relation to some superior must in fact be "without the law," be without claim for protection or justice, i. e., be outside the scope of that power which alone affords justice. Therefore the rule, *nulle terre sans seigneur*, appearing to us at first blush as an ebullition of feudal arrogance, is as a matter of fact the codification of an existing new state of law, or at the very least the clearing away of some archaic remnants, no longer to be tolerated, of the completely discarded *primitive* feudal state.

Those philosophers of history who pretend

to explain every historic development from the quality of "races," give as the center of their strategic position the alleged fact, that only the Germans, thanks to their superior "political capacity," have managed to raise the artistic edifice of the developed feudal state. Some of the vigor of this argument has departed, since the conviction began to dawn on them that in Japan, the Mongol race had accomplished this identical result. No one can tell what the negro races might have done, had not the irruption of stronger civilizations barred their way, and yet Uganda does not differ very greatly from the empires of the Carolingians or of Boleslaw the Red, except that men did not have in Uganda any "values of tradition" of mediæval culture: and these values were not any merit of the Germanic races, but a gift wherewith fortune endowed them.

Shifting the discussion from the negro to the "Semites," we find the charge made that this race has absolutely no capacity for the formation of states. And yet we find, thousands of years ago, this same feudal system developed, by Semites, if the founders of the Egyptian kingdom were Semites. One would think the following description of Thurnwald were taken from the period of the Hohenstaufen emperors: "Whoever entered the following of some powerful one, was thereafter protected by him as though he had been the head of the family. This relation . . . betokens a fiduciary relation similar to vassalage. This relation of protection in return for allegiance tends to become the basis of the organization of all Egyptian society. It is the basis of the relations of the feudal lord to his sergeants and peasants, as it is that of the Pharaoh to his officials. The cohesion of the individuals in groups subject to common protecting lords, is founded on this view, even up to the apex of the pyramid, to the king himself regarded as 'the vicar of his ancestors,' as the vassal of the gods on earth. . . . Whosoever stands without this social grasp, a 'man without a master,' is without the pale of protection and therefore without the law." [133]

The hypothesis of the endowment of any particular race has not been used by us, and we have no need of it. As Herbert Spencer says, it is the stupidest of all imaginable attempts to construct a philosophy of history.

The first characteristic of the developed feudal state is the manifold gradation of ranks built up into the one pyramid of mutual dependence. Its second distinctive mark is the amalgamation of the ethnic groups, originally separated.

The consciousness formerly existent of difference of *races* has disappeared completely. There remains only the *difference of classes*.

Henceforth we shall deal only with social classes, and no longer with ethnic groups. The social contrast is the only ruling-factor in the life of the state. Consistently with this the ethnic group consciousness changes to a class consciousness, the theories of the group, to the theories of the class. Yet they do not thereby change in the least their essence. The new dominating classes are just as full of their divine right as was the former master

group, and it soon is seen that the new nobility of the sword manages to forget, quickly
and thoroughly, its descent from the vanquished group; while the former freemen now
declassed, or the former petty nobles sunk in
the social scale, henceforth swear just as firmly
by "natural law" as did formerly only the subjected tribes.

The developed feudal state is, in its essentials, exactly the same thing as it was when
yet in the second stage of state formation. Its
form is that of dominion, its reason for being,
the political exploitation of the economic
means, limited by public law, which compels
the master class to give the correlative protection, and which guarantees to the lower class
the right of being protected, to the extent that
they are kept working and paying taxes, that
they may fulfil their duty to their masters. In
its essentials government has not changed, it
has only been disposed in more grades; and
the same applies to the exploitation, or as the
economic theory puts it, "the distribution"
of wealth.

Just as formerly, so now, the internal policy
of these states swings in that orbit prescribed
by the parallelogram of the centrifugal thrust
of the former group contests, now class wars,
counteracted by the centripetal pull of the
common interests.   Just as formerly, so now,
its foreign policy is determined by the striv-
ing of its master class for new lands and serfs,
a thrust for extension caused at the same time
by the still existing need of self-preservation.
Although differentiated much more minutely,
and integrated much more powerfully, the developed feudal state is in the end nothing more
than the primitive state arrived at its maturity.

CHAPTER VI

THE DEVELOPMENT OF THE CONSTITUTIONAL STATE

IF we understand the outcome of the feudal state, in the sense given above, as further organic development either forward or backward conditioned by the power of inner forces, but not as a physical termination, brought about or conditioned by outside forces, then we may say that the outcome of the feudal state is determined essentially by the independent development of social institutions called into being by the economic means.

Such influences may come also from without, from foreign states which, thanks to a more advanced economic development, possess a more tensely centralized power, a better military organization, and a greater forward thrust. We have touched on some of these phases. The independent development of the

Mediterranean feudal states was abruptly stopped by their collision with those maritime states, which were on a much higher plane of economic growth and wealth, and more centralized, such as Carthage, and more especially Rome. The destruction of the Persian Empire by Alexander the Great may be instanced in this connection, since Macedonia had at that time appropriated the economic advances of the Hellenic maritime states. The best example within modern times is the foreign influence in the case of Japan, whose development was shortened in an almost incredible manner by the military and peaceful impulses of Western European civilization. In the space of barely one generation it covered the road from a fully matured feudal state to the completely developed modern constitutional state.

It seems to me that we have only to deal with an abbreviation of the process of development. As far as we can see—though henceforth historical evidence becomes meager, and there are scarcely any examples from ethnography—the rule may be stated that forces from within, even without strong foreign influences, lead the matured feudal state, with strict logical consistency, on the same path to the identical conclusion.

The creators of the economic means controlling this advance are the cities and their system of money economy, which gradually supersedes the system of natural economy, and thereby dislocates the axis about which the whole life of the state swings; in place of landed property, mobile capital gradually becomes preponderant.

(a) THE EMANCIPATION OF THE PEASANTRY

All this follows as a natural consequence of the basic premise of the feudal state. The more the great private landlords become a landed nobility, the more in the same measure must the feudal system of natural economy break to pieces. The more great landed property rights become vested in and nurtured by the princes of territorial states, the more is the feudal system based on payments in kind bound to disintegrate; one may say that the two keep step in this development.

So long as the ownership of great estates is comparatively limited, the primitive principle of the bee-keeper, allowing his peasants barely enough for subsistence, can be carried out. When, however, these expand into territorial dimensions, and include, as is regularly the case, accretions of land which are the results of successful warfare, or by the relinquishment and subinfeudation through heritage or political marriages of smaller land owners, scattered widely about the country and far from the master's original domains, then the policy of the bee-keeper can no longer be carried out. Unless, therefore, the territorial magnate means to keep in his pay an immense mass of overseers, which would be both expensive and politically unwise, he would have to impose on his peasants some fixed tribute, partly rental and partly tax. The economic need of an administrative reform unites, therefore, with the political necessity, to elevate the "plebs," in the way which has already been discussed.

The more the territorial magnate ceases to be a private landlord, the more exclusively he tends to become a subject of public law, viz., prince of a territory, the more the solidarity mentioned above, between prince and people grows. We saw that some few magnates even as far back as the period of transition from great landed estates to principalities, found it to their greatest interest to carry on a "mild" government. This accomplished the result, not only of educating their plebs to a more virile consciousness toward the state, but also had the effect of making it easy for the' few remaining common freemen to give up their political rights in return for protection; while it was still more important, in that it deprived their neighbors and rivals of their precious human material. When the territorial prince has finally reached complete *de facto* independence, his self interest must prompt him steadfastly to persevere in the path thus begun. Should he, however, again invest his bailiff's or officers with lands and peasants, he will still have the most pressing political interest to see to it that his subjects are not delivered over to them without restraint.   In order to retain his control, the prince will limit the right of the "knights" to incomes from lands to definite payments in kind and limited forced labor, reserving to himself that required in the public interests, such as forced labor on highways or on bridges.   We shall soon come to see that the circumstance that in all developed feudal states the peasants have at least two masters claiming service, is decisive for their later rise.

For all these reasons, the services to be required of peasants in a developed feudal state must in some fashion be limited.   Henceforth, all surplus belongs to him free from the control of the landlord.   With this change, the character of landed property has been utterly revolutionized.   Heretofore the landlord, as of right, was entitled to the entire revenue saving only what was absolutely necessary to permit his peasants to subsist and continue their brood; while hereafter, the total product of his work, as of right, belongs to the peasant, saving only a fixed charge for his landlord as ground rent. (The possession of vast landed estates has developed into (*manorial*) *rights.* *This completes the second important step taken by humanity toward its goal.* The first step was taken when man made the transition from the stage of bear to that of the bee-keeper, and thereby discovered slavery; this step abolishes slavery.   Laboring human-ity, heretofore only *an object* of the law, now for the first time becomes an entity capable of enjoying rights. The *labor motor,* with-out rights, belonging to its master, and with-out effective guarantees of life and limb, has now become the taxpaying subject of some prince.   Henceforth the economic means, now for the first time assured of its success, develops its forces quite differently.   The peasant works with incomparably more in-dustry and care, obtains more than he needs, and thereby calls into being the "city" in the economic sense of the term, viz., the industrial city. The surplus produced by the peasantry calls into being a demand for objects not produced in the peasant economy; while at the same time, the more intensive agriculture brings about a reduction of those industrial by-products heretofore worked out by the peasant house industry.

Since agriculture and cattle-raising absorb in ever increasing degrees the energies of the rural family, it becomes possible and necessary to divide labor between original production and manufacture; the village tends to become primarily the place of the former, the industrial city comes into being as the seat of the latter.

(b) THE GENESIS OF THE INDUSTRIAL STATE

Let there be no misunderstanding: we do not maintain that the city comes thus into being, but only the *industrial city*. There has been in existence the real historical city, to be found in every developed feudal state. Such cities came into being either because of a purely political means, as a stronghold,[134] or by the coöperation of the political with economic means, *as a market place*, or because of some religious need, as the environs of some temple.* Wherever such a city in the historical sense exists in the neighborhood, the newly arising industrial city tends to grow up about it; otherwise it develops spontaneously from the existing and matured division of labor. As a rule, it will in its turn grow into a stronghold and have its own places of worship.

These are but accidental historical admixtures. In its strict economic sense "city" means the place of the economic means, or the exchange and interchange for equivalent values between rural production and manufacture. This corresponds to the common use of language, by which a stronghold however great, an agglomeration of temples, cloisters

---

* "Every place of worship gathers about it dwellings of the priests, schools, and rest-houses for pilgrims."—Ratzel, l. c. II., p. 575.

Naturally, every place toward which great pilgrimages proceed becomes an extended trade center. We may see the remembrances thereof in the fact that the great wholesale markets, held at stated times in Northern Europe, are called *Messen* from the religious ceremony.

and places of pilgrimage however extensive, were they conceivable without any place for exchange, would be designated after their external characteristics as "like a city" or "resembling a city."

Although there may have been few changes in the exterior of the historical city, there has taken place an internal revolution on a magnificent scale. *The industrial city is directly opposed to the state.* As the state is the developed political means, *so the industrial city is the developed economic means.* The great contest filling universal history, nay its very meaning, henceforth takes place between city and state.

The city as an economic, political body undermines the feudal system with political and economic arms. With the first the city *forces,* with the second it *lures,* their power away from the feudal master class.

This process takes place in the field of politics by the interference of the city, now a center of its own powers, in the political mechanism of the developed feudal state, between the central power and the local territorial magnates and their subjects. The cities are the strongholds and the dwelling places of warlike men, as well as depots of material for carrying on war (arms, etc.); and later they become central supply reservoirs for money used in the contests between the central government and the growing territorial princes, or between these in their internecine wars. Thus they are important strategic points or valuable allies; and may by far-sighted policy acquire important rights.

As a rule, the cities take the part of the crown in fights against the feudal nobles, from social reasons, because the landed nobles refuse to recognize the social equality, demanded as of right by their more wealthy citizens; from political reasons, because the central government, thanks to the solidarity between prince and people, is more apt to be influenced by common interests than is the territorial magnate, who serves only his private interests; and finally from economic reasons, because city life can prosper only in peace and safety.

The practises of chivalry, such as club law, and private warfare, and the knights' practise of looting caravans are irreconcilable with the economic means; and therefore, the cities are faithful allies of the guardians of peace and justice, first to the emperor, later on, to the sovereign territorial prince; and when the armed citizenship breaks and pillages some robber baron's fortress, the tiny drop reflects the identical process happening in the ocean of history.

In order successfully to carry this political rôle the city must attract as many citizens as possible, an endeavor also forced on it by purely economic considerations, since both divisions of labor and wealth increase with increased citizenship. Therefore cities favor immigration with all their powers; and once more show in this the polar contrast of their essential difference from the feudal landlords. The new citizens thus attracted into the cities are withdrawn from the feudal estates, which are thereby weakened in power of taxation and military defense in proportion as the cities are strengthened. The city becomes a mighty competitor at the auction, wherein the serf is knocked down to the highest bidder, to the one, that is to say, who offers the most rights. The city offers the peasant *complete liberty,* and in some cases house and courtyard. The principle, "city air frees the peasant" is successfully fought out; and the central government, pleased to strengthen the cities and to weaken the turbulent nobles, usually confirms by charter the newly acquired rights.

The third great move in the progress of universal history is to be seen in the discovery of the honor of free labor; or better in its rediscovery, it having been lost sight of since those far-off times in which the free huntsman and the subjugated primitive tiller enjoyed the results of their labor. As yet the peasant bears the mark of the pariah and his rights are little respected. But in the wall-girt, well-defended city, the citizen holds his head high. He is a freeman in every sense of the word, free even at law, since we find in the grants of rights to many early enfranchised cities

(*Ville-franche*) the provision that a serf residing therein "a year and a day" undisturbed by his master's claim is to be deemed free.

Within the city walls there are still various ranks and grades of political status. At first the old settlers, the men of rank equal with the nobles of the surrounding country, the ancient freemen of the burgh, refuse to the newcomers, usually poor artisans or hucksters, the right of sharing in the government. But, as we saw in the case of the maritime cities, such gradations of rank can not be maintained within a business community. The majority, intelligent, skeptical, closely organized and compact, forces the concession of equal rights. The only difference is that the contest is longer in a developed feudal state, because now the fight concerns not only the parties at interest. The great territorial magnates of the neighborhood and the princes hinder the full development of the forces by their interference. In the maritime states of the ancient world, there was no *tertius gaudens* who could derive any profit from the contests within the city, since outside the cities there existed no system of powerful feudal lords.

These then, are the political arms of the cities in their contest with the feudal state: alliances with the crown, direct attack, and the enticing away of the serfs of the feudal lords into the enfranchising air of the city. Its economic weapons are no less effective, the change from payments in kind to the system of *money as a means of exchange* is inseparably connected with civic methods, is the means whereby the method of payment in kind is utterly destroyed, and with it the feudal state.

(c) THE INFLUENCES OF MONEY ECONOMY

The sociological process set into motion by the system of money economy is so well known and its mechanics are so generally recognized, that a few suggestions will suffice.

Here, as in the case of the maritime states, the consequence of the invading money system is that the *central government becomes almost omnipotent, while the local powers are reduced to complete impotence.*

Dominion is not an end in itself, but merely the means of the rulers to their essential object, the enjoyment without labor of articles of consumption as many and as valuable as possible. During the prevalence of the system of natural economy there is no other way of obtaining them save by dominion; the wardens of the marches and the territorial princes obtain their wealth by their political power. The more peasants who are owned, the greater is the military power and the larger the scope of the territory subjected, and thus the greater are the revenues. As soon, however, as the products of agriculture are exchangeable for enticing wares, it becomes more rational for every one primarily a private man, i. e., for every feudal lord not a territorial prince—and this now includes the knights—to decrease as far as possible the number of peasants, and to leave only such small numbers as can with the utmost labor turn out the greatest product from the land, and to leave these as little as possible. The net product of the real estate, thus tremendously increased, is now taken to the markets and sold for goods, and is no longer used to keep a fencible body of guards. Having dissolved this following, the knight becomes simply the manager of a knight's fee.* With this event, as with one blow, the central power, that of king or territorial prince, is without a rival for the dominion, and has become politically omnipotent. The unruly vassals, who formerly made the weak kings tremble, after a short attempt at joint rule during the time of the government of the feudal estates, have changed into the supple courtiers, begging favors at the hands of some absolute monarch, like Louis XIV. And he furthermore has become their last resort, since the military power, now solely exercised by him as the paymaster of the forces, alone can protect them from the ever-immanent revolt of their tenants, ground to the bone. While in the time of natural economy the crown was in nearly every instance allied with peasants and cities against nobility, we now have the

* See reference as to the meaning of *Rittergutsbesitz*, ante, page 84.—*Translator*.

union of the absolute kings, born from the feudal state, with their nobility, against the representatives of the economic means.

Since the days of Adam Smith it has been customary to state this fundamental revolution in some such form, as though the foolish nobles had sold their birthright for a mess of pottage, when they traded their dominion for foolish articles of luxury. No view can be more erroneous. (Individuals often err in the safe-guarding of their interests: *a class for any prolonged period never is in error.*)

The fact of the matter is, that the system of money payments strengthened the central power so mightily and immediately, that even without the interposition of the agrarian upheaval, any resistance of the landed nobility would have been senseless. As is shown in the history of antiquity, the army of a central government, financially strong, is always superior to feudal levies. Money permits the armament of peasant sons, and the drilling of them into professional soldiers, whose solid organization is always superior to the loose con-

federation of an armed mass of knights.
Besides, at this stage, the central government
could also count on the aid of the well-armed
squares of the urban guilds.

Gunpowder did the rest in Western Europe. Firearms, however, are a product that
can be turned out only in the industrial estab-
lishments of a wealthy city. Because of these
technical military reasons, even that feudal
landlord who might not care for the newly
established luxuries and who might only be
desirous of maintaining or increasing his independent position, must subject his territories to the same agrarian revolution; since,
in order to be strong, he now before all else
must have *money,* which in the new order of
things, has become the *nervus rerum,* either to
buy arms or to engage mercenaries. A
second capitalistic wholesale undertaking,
therefore, has come into being through the
system of payments in money; besides the
wholesale management of landed estates, war
is carried on as a great business enterprise—
the condottieri appear on the stage. The mar-

ket is full of material for armies of mercenaries, the discharged guards of the feudal
lords and the young peasants whose lands have
been taken up by the lords.

There are instances where some petty noble
may mount to the throne of some territorial
principality, as happened many a time in
Italy, and as was accomplished by Albrecht
Wallenstein, even as late as the period of the
Thirty Years' War. But that is a matter of
individual fate, not affecting the final result.
The local powers disappear from the contest
of political forces as independent centers of
authority and retain the remnant of their
former influence only so long as they serve the
princes as a source of supplies; that is, the
state composed of its feudal estates.

The infinite increase in the power of the
crown is then enhanced by a second creation
of the system of payment in money, by
officialdom. We have told in detail of the
vicious circle which forced the feudal state into
a cul-de-sac between agglomeration and dissolution, as long as its bailiffs had to be paid

with "lands and peasants" and thereby were nursed into potential rivals of their creator. With the advent of payments in money, the vicious circle is broken. Henceforth the central government carries on its functions through paid employees, permanently dependent on their paymaster.[135] Henceforth there is possible a permanently established, tensely centralized government, and empires come into being, such as had not existed since the developed maritime states of antiquity, which also were founded on the payments in money.

This revolution of the political mechanism was everywhere put into motion by the development of the money economy—with but one exception, as far as I can see, viz., Egypt.

Here, according to the statement of experts, no definite information is to be had, and it seems that the system of money exchanges appears as a matured institution only in Greek times. Until that time, the tribute of the peasants was paid in kind;[136] and yet we find, shortly after the expulsion of the Shepherd

Kings, during the New Empire (*circa* sixteenth century B. C.), that the absolutism of the kings was fully developed: "The military power is upheld by foreign mercenaries, the administration is carried on by a *centralized body of officials* dependent on the royal favor, *while the feudal aristocracy has disappeared.*" [137]

It may seem that this exception proves the rule. Egypt is a country of exceptional geographic conformation. Jammed into a narrow compass, between mountains and the desert, a natural highway, the River Nile, traverses its entire length, and permits the transportation of bulky freight with much greater facility than the finest road. And this highway made it easy for the Pharaoh to assemble the taxes of all his districts in his own storehouses, the so-called "houses" [138] and from them to supply his garrisons and civil employees with the products themselves *in natura*. For that reason Egypt, after it has once become unified into an empire, stays centralized, until foreign powers extinguish its life as a "state." "This circumstance is the source of the enormous and plenary power exercised by the Pharaoh where payments are still made in kind; the exclusive and immediate control of the objects of daily consumption are in his hand. The ruler distributes to his employees only such quantities of the entire mass of goods as appears to him good and proper; and since the articles of luxury are nearly all exclusively in his hands, he enjoys on this account also an extraordinary plenitude of power." [139]

With this one exception, where a mighty force executes the task, the power of circulating money seems in all cases to have dissolved the feudal state.

The cost of the revolution fell on peasants and cities. When peace is made, the crown and the petty nobles mutually sacrifice the peasantry, dividing them, so to say, into two ideal halves; the crown grants to the nobility the major part of the peasants' common lands, and the greatest part of their working powers that are not yet expropriated; the nobility

concedes to the crown the right of recruiting
and of taxing both peasantry and cities. The
peasant, who had grown wealthy in freedom,
sinks back into poverty and therefore into
social inferiority. The former feudal powers
now unite as allies to subjugate the cities, except where, as in Upper Italy, these become
feudal central powers themselves. (And even
in that case they for the most part all fall into
the power of captains of mercenaries, condottieri.) The power of attack of the adversaries has become stronger, the power of
the cities has diminished. For with the decay
of the peasantry, their purchase power di-
minishes and with it the prosperity of the
cities, based thereon. The small cities in the
country stagnate and become poorer, and being now incapable of defense, fall a prey to the
absolutist rule of the territorial princes; the
larger cities, where the demand for the luxuries
of the nobles has brought into being a strong
trading element, split up into social groups and
thus fritter away their political strength.
The immigration now pouring into their walls

is composed of discharged and broken mercenaries, dispossessed peasants, pauperized mechanics from the smaller towns; it is in other words a *proletarian* immigration. For the first time there appears, in the terminology of Karl Marx, the "free laborer," in masses, competing with his own class in the labor markets of the cities.   And again, the "law of agglomeration" enters to form effective class and property distinctions, and thus to tear apart the civic population. Wild fights take place in the cities between the classes; through which the territorial prince, in nearly every instance, again succeeds in gaining control.   The only cities that can permanently escape the deadly embrace of the prince's power are the few genuine "maritime states," or "city states."

As in the case of the maritime states, the pivot of the state's life has again shifted over to another place.   Instead of circling about wealth vested in landed estates, it now turns about capitalized wealth, because in the meantime property in real estate has itself become "capital." *Why is it that the development does not, as in the case of the maritime states, open out into the capitalistic expropriation of slave labor?*

There are two controlling reasons, one internal, the other external. The external reason is to be found in this, that slave hunting on a profitable scale is scarcely possible at this time in any part of the world, since nearly all countries within reach are also organized as strong states. Wherever it is possible, as for instance, in the American colonies of the West European powers, it develops at once.

The internal reason may be found in the circumstance that the peasant of the interior countries, in contrast to the conditions prevailing in the maritime states, is subject, not to one master, but to at least two * persons entitled to his service, his prince and his landlord. Both resist any attempt to diminish their peasants' capacity for service, since this is essential to their interests. Especially strong princes did much for their peasants, e. g., those of

---

* In mediæval Germany the peasants pay tribute in many cases not only to the landlord and to the territorial prince, but also to the provost and to the bailiff.

Brandenburg-Prussia. For this reason, the peasants, although exploited miserably, yet retained their personal liberty and their standing as subjects endowed with personal rights in all states where the feudal system had been fully developed when the system of payments in money replaced that of payments in kind.

The evidence that this explanation is correct may be found in the relations of those states which were gripped by the system of exchange in money, before the feudal system had become worked out.

This applies especially to those districts of Germany formerly occupied by Slavs, but particularly to *Poland*. In these districts, the feudal system had not yet been worked out as thoroughly as in the regions where the demand for grain products in the great western industrial centers had changed the nobles, the subjects of public law, into the owners of a *Rittergut*,* the subjects of private economic interests. In these districts, the peasants were subject to the duty of rendering service only to

* See foot-note on page 84.

one master, who was both their liege lord and
landlord; and because of that, there came into
being the republics of nobles mentioned above,
which, as far as the pressure of their more progressed neighbors would permit, tended to ap-
proach the capitalistic system of exploiting of
slave labor.[140]

The following is so well known that it can
be stated briefly. [The system of exchange by
means of money matures into capitalism, and
brings into being new classes in juxtaposition
to the landowners; the capitalist demands
equal rights with the formerly privileged
orders, and finally obtains them by revolution-
izing the lower plebs. In this attack on the
sacredly established order of things, the cap-
italists unite with the lower classes, naturally
under the banner of "natural law." But as
soon as the victory has been achieved, the class
based on movable wealth, the so-called middle
class, turns its arms on the lower classes, makes
peace with its former opponents, and invokes in
its reactionary fight on the proletarians, its late
allies, the theory of legitimacy, or makes use

of an evil mixture of arguments based partly on legitimacy and partly on pseudo-liberalism.

In this manner the state has gradually matured from the primitive robber state, through the stages of the developed feudal state, through absolutism, to the modern constitutional state.

(d) THE MODERN CONSTITUTIONAL STATE

Let us give the mechanics and kinetics of the modern state a moment's time.

In principle, it is the same entity as the primitive robber state or the developed feudal state. There has been added, however, one new element—*officialdom*, which at least will have this object, that in the contest of the various classes, it will represent the common interests of the state as a whole. In how far this purpose is subserved we shall investigate in another place. Let us at this time study the state in respect to those characteristics which it has brought over from its youthful stages.

Its *form* still continues to be domination, its content still remains the exploitation of the economic means. The latter continues to be limited by public law, which on the one hand protects the traditional "distribution" of the total products of the nation; while on the other it attempts to maintain at their full efficiency the taxpayers and those bound to render service. The internal policy of the state continues to revolve in the path prescribed for it by the parallelogram of the centrifugal force of class contests and the centripetal impulse of the common interests in the state; and its foreign policy continues to be determined by the interests of the master class, now comprising besides the landed also the moneyed interests.

In principle, there are now, as before, only two classes to be distinguished: one a ruling class, which acquires more of the total product of the labor of the people—the economic means—than it has contributed, and a subject class, which obtains less of the resultant wealth than it has contributed. Each of these classes, in turn, depending on the degree of economic development, is divided into more or fewer subclasses or strata, which grade off according to the fortune or misfortune of their economic standards.

Among highly developed states there is found introduced between the two principal classes a transitional class, which also may be subdivided into various strata. Its members are bound to render service to the upper class, while they are entitled to receive service from the classes below them. To illustrate with an example, we find in the ruling class in modern Germany at least three strata. First come the great landed magnates, who at the same time are the principal shareholders in the larger industrial undertakings and mining companies: next stand the captains of industry and the "bankocrats," who also in many cases have become owners of great estates. In consequence of this they quickly amalgamate with the first layer. Such, for example, are the Princes Fugger, who were formerly bankers of Augsburg, and the Counts of Donnersmarck, owners of extensive mines in Silesia. And finally there are the petty country nobles, whom we shall hereafter term *junker* or "squires."

The subject class, at all events, consists of petty peasants, agricultural laborers, factory and mine hands, with small artisans and subordinate officials. The "middle classes" are the classes of the transition: composed of the owners of large and medium-sized farms, the small manufacturers, and the best paid mechanics, besides those rich "bourgeois," such as Jews, who have not become rich enough to overcome certain traditional difficulties which oppose their arrival at the stage of intermarriage with the upper class. All these render unrequited service to the upper class, and receive unrequited service from the lower classes. This determines the result which occurs either to the stratum as a whole or to the individuals in it; that is to say, either a complete acceptance into the upper class, or an absolute sinking into the lower class. Of the (German) transitional classes, the large farmers and the manufacturers of average wealth have risen, while the majority of artisans have descended to the lower classes. We have thus arrived at the kinetics of classes.

The interests of every class set in motion an actual body of associated forces, which impel it with a definite momentum toward the attainment of a definite goal. [All classes whatever have the same goal; viz., the total result of the productive labor of all the denizens of a given state. Every class attempts to obtain as large a share as possible of the national production; and since all strive for identically the same object, the *class contest* results. This contest of classes is the content of all history of states, except in so far as the interest of the state as a whole produces common actions. These we may at this point disregard, since they have been given undue prominence by the traditional method of historical study, and lead to onesided views. Historically this class contest is shown to be a *party fight*. A party is originally and in its essence nothing save an organized representation of a class. Wherever a class, by reason of social differentiation, has split up into numerous sub-classes with varied separate interests, the party claiming to represent it disintegrates at the earliest opportunity into a mass of tiny parties, and these will either be allies or mortal enemies according to the degree of divergence of the class interests. Where on the other hand a former class contrast has disappeared by social differentiation, the two former parties amalgamate in a short time into a new party. As an example of the first case we may recall the splitting off of the artisans and Anti-Semite parties from the party of German Liberalism, as a consequence of the fact that the first represented descending groups, while the latter represented ascending ones. A characteristic example of the second category may be found in the political amalgamation which bound together into the farmers' union the petty landed squires of the East Elbian country with West Elbian rich peasants on large plantations. Since the petty squire sinks and the farmer rises, they meet half-way. All party policy can have but one meaning, viz., to procure for the class represented as great a share as is possible of the total national production. In other words, the pre-

ferred classes intend to maintain their share, at
the very least, at the ancient scale, and if possible, to increase it toward such a maximum
as shall permit the exploited classes just a bare
existence, to keep them fit to do their work,
just as in the bee-keeper stages.   Their object
is to confiscate the entire surplus product of the
economic means, a surplus which increases
enormously as population becomes more dense
and division of labor more specialized.   On the
other hand, the group of exploited classes
would like to reduce their tribute to the zero-
point, and to consume the entire product themselves; and the transitional classes work as much
as possible toward the reduction of their tribute
to the upper classes, while at the same time they
strive to increase their unrequited income from
the classes underneath.

This is the aim and the content of all party
contests.   The ruling class conducts this fight
with all those means which its acquired dominion has handed down to it.   In consequence of this, the ruling class sees to it that

legislation is framed in its interest and to serve its purpose—class legislation. These laws are then applied in such wise that the blunted back of the sword of justice is turned upward, while its sharpened edge is turned downward—class justice. The governing class in every state uses the administration of the state in the interest of those belonging to it under a twofold aspect. In the first place it reserves to its adherents all prominent places and all offices of influence and of profit, in the army, in the superior branches of government service, and in places on the bench; and secondly, by these very agencies, it directs the entire policy of the state, causes its class-politics to bring about commercial wars, colonial policies, protective tariffs, legislation in some degree improving the conditions of the laboring classes, electoral reform policies, etc. As long as the nobles ruled the state, they exploited it as they would have managed an estate; when the bourgeoisie obtain the mastery, the state is exploited as though it were a factory. And the class-religion covers all defects, as long as they can be endured, with its "don't touch the foundation of society."

There still exist in the public law a number of political privileges and economic strategic positions, which favor the master class: such as, in Prussia, a system of voting which gives the plutocrats an undue advantage over the less favored classes, a limitation of the constitutional rights of free assembly, regulations for servants, etc. For that reason, the *constitutional fight*, carried on over thousands of years and dominating the life of the state, is still uncompleted. The fight for improved conditions of life, another phase of the party and class struggle, usually takes place in the halls of legislative bodies, but often it is carried on by means of demonstrations in the streets, by general strikes, or by open outbreaks.

But the plebs have finally and definitely learned that these remnants of feudal strategic centers, do not, except in belated instances, constitute the final stronghold of their opponents. It is not in political, but rather in economic conditions that the cause must be sought, which has brought it about that even in the modern constitutional state, the "distribution of wealth" has not been changed in principle. Just as in feudal times, the great mass of men live in bitter poverty; even under the best conditions, they have the meager necessities of life, earned by hard, crushing, stupefying forced labor, no longer exacted by right of political exploitation, but just as effectively forced from the laborers by their economic needs. And just as before in the un-reformed days, the narrow minority, a new master class, a conglomerate of holders of ancient privileges and of newly rich, gathers in the tribute, now grown to immensity; and not only does not render any service therefor, but flaunts its wealth in the face of labor by riotous living. The class contest henceforth is devoted more and more to these economic causes, based on vicious systems of distribution; and it takes shape in a hand-to-hand fight between exploiters and proletariat, carried on by strikes, coöperative societies and trades unions. The economic organization first forces recognition, and then equal rights; then it leads and finally

controls the political destinies of the labor
party. In the end therefore the trade union
controls the party. Thus far the development
of the state has progressed in Great Britain
and in the United States. *No. Our unions don't enter political ring.*

Were it not that there has been added to the
modern state an entirely new element, its
officialdom, the constitutional state, though *Ora thyloni*
more finely differentiated and more power-
fully integrated, would, so far as form and *Oh yes*
content go, be little different from its proto- *You bet they do*
types.

As a matter of principle, the state officials, *I'll add a yes.*
paid from the funds of the state, are removed *Another*
from the economic fights of conflicting inter- *yes —*
ests; and therefore it is rightly considered un- *consider*
becoming for any one in the service of the *"volun-*
government to be taking part in any money *tary"*
making undertaking, and in no well ordered *# 1*
bureaucracy is it tolerated. Were it possible *e in him.*
ever thoroughly to realize the principle, and *times in*
did not every official, even the best of them, *the Cl*
bring with him that concept of the state held by *tw presi*
the class from which he originated, one would *kentied*
find in officialdom, as a matter of fact, that *el*

+ also legislation support of c — limiting ec service elect

moderating and order making force, removed
from the conflict of class interests, whereby the
state might be led toward its new goal. It
would become the fulcrum of Archimedes
whence the world of the state might be moved.

But the principle, we are sorry to say, can
not be carried out completely; and furthermore, the officials do not cease being real men,
do not become mere abstractions without class-
consciousness. This may be quite apart from
the fact that, in Europe at least, a participa-
tion in a definite form of undertakings—viz.,
handling large landed estates—is regarded as
a favorable means of getting on in the service
of the state, and will continue to be so as long
as the landed nobility preponderates. In consequence of this, many officials on the Continent, and one may even say the most influ-
ential officials, are subject to pressure by
enormous economic interests; and are uncon-
sciously, and often against their will, brought
into the class contests.

There are factors, such as extra allowances
made by either fathers or fathers-in-law, or

hereditary estates, and affinity to the persons in control of the landed and moneyed interest or allied with them, whereby the solidarity of interest among the ruling class is if anything increased from the fact that these officials, practically without exception, are taken from a class with whom since their boyhood days they have been on terms of intimacy. Were there, however, no such unity of economic interests the demeanor of the officials would be influenced entirely by the pure interests of the state.

For this reason, as a rule, the most efficient, most objective and most impartial set of officials is found in poor states. Prussia, for example, was formerly indebted to its poverty for that incomparable body of officials who handled it through all its troubles. These employees of the state were actually, in consonance with the rule laid down above, dissociated completely from all interests in money making, directly or indirectly.

This ideal body of officials is a rare occurrence in the more wealthy states. The plutocratic development draws the individual more and more into its vortex, robbing him of his objectivity and of his impartiality. [And yet the officials continue to fulfil the duty which the modern state requires of them, to preserve the interests of the state as opposed to the interests of any class. And this interest is preserved by them, even though against their will, or at least without clear consciousness of the fact, in such manner that the economic means, which called the bureaucracy into being, is in the end advanced on its tedious path of victory, as against the political means. No one doubts that the officials carry on class politics, prescribed for them by the constellation of forces operating in the state; and to that extent, they certainly do represent the master class from which they sprang. But they do ameliorate the bitterness of the struggle, by opposing the extremists in either camp, and by advocating amendments to existing law, when the social development has become ripened for their enactment, without waiting until the contest over these has become acute. Where an efficient race of princes governs, whose momentary representative adopts the policy of King Frederick, which was to regard himself only as "the first servant of the state," what has been said above applies to him in an increased degree, all the more so as his interests, as the permanent beneficiary of the continued existence of the state, would before all else prompt him to strengthen the centripetal forces and to weaken the centrifugal powers. ⌈In the course of the preceding we have in many instances noted the natural solidarity between prince and people, as an historic force of great value. In the completed constitutional state, in which the monarch in but an infinitesimally small degree is a subject of private economic interests, he tends to be almost completely "an official." This community of interests is emphasized here much more strongly than in either the feudal state or the despotically governed state, where the dominion, at least for one-half its extent, is based on the private economic interests of the prince.

Even in a constitutional state, the outer form

of government is not the decisive factor; the fight of the classes is carried on and leads to the same result in a republic as in a monarchy. In spite of this, it must be admitted that there is more probability, that, other things being equal, the curve of development of the state in a monarchy will be more sweeping, with less secondary incurvity, because the prince is less affected by momentary losses of popularity, is not so sensitive to momentary gusts of disapproval, as is a president elected for a short term of years, and he can therefore shape his policies for longer periods of time.

We must not fail to mention a special form of officialdom, the scientific staffs of the universities, whose influence on the upward development of the state must not be underestimated. Not only is this a creation of the economic means, as were the officials themselves, but it at the same time represents an historical force, *the need of causality,* which we found heretofore only as an ally of the conquering state. We saw that this need created superstition while the state was on a primitive stage; its bastard, the taboo, we found in all cases to be an effective means of control by the master class. From these same needs then, *science* was developed, attacking and destroying superstition, and thereby assisting in preparation of the path of evolution. That is the incalculable historical service of science and especially of the universities.

CHAPTER VII

THE TENDENCY OF THE DEVELOPMENT OF THE STATE

WE have endeavored to discover the development of the state from its most remote past up to present times, following its course like an explorer, from its source down the streams to its effluence in the plains. Broad and powerfully its waves roll by, until it disappears into the mist of the horizon, into unexplored and, for the present-day observer, undiscoverable regions.

Just as broadly and powerfully the stream of history—and until the present day all history has been the history of states—rolls past our view, and the course thereof is covered by the blanketing fogs of the future. Shall we dare to set up hypotheses concerning the future course, until "with unrestrained joy he sinks into the arms of his waiting, expectant father"?

(Goethe's *Prometheus.*) Is it possible to establish a scientifically founded prognosis in regard to the future development of the state?

I believe in this possibility. The tendency[141] of state development unmistakably leads to one point: seen in its essentials the state will cease to be the "developed political means" and will become "a freemen's citizenship." In other words, its outer shell will remain in essentials the form which was developed in the constitutional state, under which the administration will be carried on by an officialdom. But the content of the states heretofore known will have changed its vital element by the disappearance of the economic exploitation of one class by another. And since the state will, by this, come to be without either classes or class interests, the bureaucracy of the future will truly have attained that ideal of the impartial guardian of the common interests, which nowadays it laboriously attempts to reach. The "state" of the future will be "society" guided by self-government.

Libraries full of books have been written

on the delimitation of the concepts "state" and "society." The problem, however, from our point of view has an easy solution. | The "state" is the fully developed political means, society the fully developed economic means. Heretofore state and society were indissolubly intertwined: in the "freemen's citizenship," there will be no "state" but only "society." |

This prognosis of the future development of the state contains by inclusion all of those famous formulæ, whereby the great philosophical historians have endeavored to determine the "resulting value" of universal history. It contains the "progress from warlike activity to peaceful labor" of St. Simon, as well as Hegel's "development from slavery to free- dom"; the "evolution of humanity" of Herder, as well as "the penetration of reason through nature" of Schleiermacher.

Our times have lost the glad optimism of the classical and of the humanist writers; sociologic pessimism rules the spirit of these latter days. The prognosis here stated can not as yet claim to have many adherents. Not only do the persons obtaining the profits of dominion, thanks to their obsession by their class spirit, regard it as an incredible concept; those belonging to the subjugated class as well regard it with the utmost skepticism. It is true that the proletarian theory, as a matter of principle, predicts identically the same result. But the adherents of that theory do not believe it possible by the path of evolution but only through revolution. It is then thought of as a picture of a "society" varying in all respects from that evolved by the progress of history; in other words, as an organization of the economic means, as a system of economics without competition and market, as collectivism. The anarchistic theory makes form and content of the "state" as inseparable as heads and tails of the coin; no "government" without exploitation! It would therefore smash both the form and the content of the state, and thus bring on a condition of anarchy, even if thereby all the economic advantages of a division of labor should have to be sacrificed. Even so great a thinker as the late Ludwig Gumplowicz, who first laid the foundation on which the present theory of the state has been developed, is a sociological pessimist; and from the same reasons as are the anarchists, whom he combated so violently. He too regards as eternally inseparable form and content, government and class-exploitation; since he however, and I think correctly, does not consider it possible that many people may live together without some coercive force vested in some government, he declares the class-state to be an "immanent" and not only an historical category.

Only a small fraction of social liberals, or of liberal socialists, believe in the evolution of a society without class dominion and class exploitation which shall guarantee to the individual, besides political, also economic liberty of movement, within of course the limitations of the economic means. That was the *credo* of the old social liberalism, of pre-Manchester days, enunciated by Quesnay and especially by Adam Smith, and again taken up in modern times by Henry George and Theodore Hertzka.

This prognosis may be substantiated in two ways, one through history and philosophy, the other by political economy, as a tendency of the development of the state, and as a tendency of the evolution of economics, both clearly tending toward *one* point.

The tendency of the *development of the state* was shown in the preceding as a steady and victorious combat of economic means against political means. We saw that, in the beginning, the right to the economic means, the right to equality and to peace, was restricted to the tiny circle of the horde bound together by ties of blood, an endowment from pre-human conditions of society;[142] while without the limits of this isle of peace raged the typhoon of the political means. But we saw expanding more and more the circles from which the laws of peace crowded out their adversary, and everywhere we saw their advance connected with the advance of the economic means, of the barter of groups for equivalents, amongst one another. The first exchange may have been the exchange of fire, then the barter of women, and finally the exchange of goods, the domain of peace constantly extending its borders.   It protected the market places, then the streets leading to them, and finally it protected the merchants traveling on these streets.

In the course of this discussion it was shown how the "state" absorbed and developed these organizations making for peace, and how in consequence these drive back ever further right based on mere might.   Merchants' law becomes city law; the industrial city, the developed economic means, undermines the feudal state, the developed political means; and finally the civic population, in open fight, annihilates the political remnants of the feudal state, and re-conquers for the entire population of the state freedom and right to equality, *urban* law becomes public law and finally international law.

Furthermore, on no horizon can be seen any force now capable of resisting effectively this heretofore efficient tendency.   On the contrary, the interference of the past, which temporarily blocked the process, is obviously becoming weaker and weaker. The international relations of commerce and trade acquired among the nations a preponderating importance over the diminishing warlike and political relations; and in the intra-national sphere, by reason of the same process of economic development, movable capital, the creation of the right to peace, preponderates in ever increasing measure over landed property rights, the creation of the right of war. At the same time superstition more and more loses its influence. And therefore one is justified in concluding that the tendency so marked will work out to its logical end, excluding the political means and all its works, until the complete victory of the economic means is attained.

But it may be objected that in the modern constitutional state all the more prominent remnants of the antique law of war have already been chiseled out.

On the contrary, there survives a considerable remnant of these institutions, masked it is true in economic garb, and apparently no longer a legal privilege but only economic right, *the ownership of large estates—the first creation and the last stronghold of the political means.* Its mask has preserved it from under-going the fate of all other feudal creations. And yet this last remnant of the right of war is doubtless the last unique obstacle in the path-way of humanity; and doubtless the *development of economics* is on its way to destroy it.

To substantiate these remarks I must refer the reader to other books, wherein I have given the detailed evidence of the above and can not in the space allotted here repeat it at large.[143] I can only re-state the principal points made in these books.

There is no difference in principle between the distribution of the total products of the economic means among the separate classes of a constitutional state, the so-called "capitalistic distribution," from that prevailing in the feudal state.

All the more important economic schools coincide in finding the cause in this, that the supply of "free" laborers (i. e., according to

Karl Marx politically free and economically without capital) perpetually exceeds the demand, and that hence there exists "the social relation of capital." There "are constantly two laborers running after one master for work, and lowering, for one another, the wages"; and therefore the "surplus value" remains with the capitalist class, while the laborer never gets a chance to form capital for himself and to become an employer.

Whence comes this surplus supply of free laborers?

The explanation of the "bourgeois" theory, according to which this surplus supply is caused by the overproduction of children by proletarian parents, is based on a logical fallacy, and is contradicted by all known facts.[144]

The explanation of the proletarian theory according to which the capitalistic process of production itself produces the "free laborers," by setting up again and again new labor-saving machines, is also based on a logical fallacy and is likewise contradicted by all known facts.[145]

The evidence of all facts shows rather, and the conclusion may be deduced without fear of contradiction, *that the oversupply of "free laborers" is descended from the right of holding landed property in large estates;* and that emigration into towns and oversea from these landed properties are the causes of the capitalistic distribution. •

Doubtless there is a growing tendency in economic development whereby the ruin of vast landed estates will be accomplished. The system is their bleeding to death, without hope of salvation, caused by the freedom of the former serfs—the necessary consequence of the development of the cities. As soon as the peasants had obtained the right of moving about without their landlords' passport (German *Freizuegigkeit*), there developed the chance of escape from the countries which formerly oppressed them. The system of emigration created "the competition from oversea," together with the fall, on the Continent, of prices for farm products, and made necessary perpetually rising wages. By these two factors ground rent is reduced from two sides, and must gradually sink to the zero point, since here too no counterforce is to be recognized whereby the process might be diverted.[146] Thus the system of vast territorial estates falls apart. When, however, it has disappeared, there can be no oversupply of "free laborers." On the contrary "two masters will run after one laborer and must raise the price on themselves." There will be no "surplus value" for the capitalist class, because the laborer himself can form capital and himself become an employer. By this the last remaining vestige of the political means will have been destroyed, and economic means alone will exercise sway. The *content* of such a society is the "pure economics" [147] of the equivalent exchange of commodities against commodities, or of labor force against commodities, and the political *form* of this society will be the "freemen's citizenship."

This theoretical deduction is moreover confirmed by the *experience of history*. Wherever there existed a society in which vast estates did not exist to draw an increasing rental, there "pure economics" existed, and society approximated the form of the state to that of the "freemen's citizenship."

Such a community was found in the Germany of the four centuries [148] from about A. D. 1000, when the primitive system of vast estates was developed into the socially harmless dominion over vast territories, until about the year 1400, when the newly arisen great properties, created by the political means, the robber wars in the countries formerly Slavic, shut the settlers from the westward out of lands eastward of the Elbe.[149]   Such a community was the Mormon state of Utah, which has not been greatly changed in this respect, where a wise land legislation permitted only small and moderate sized farm holdings.[150]   Such a community was to be found in the city and county of Vineland, Iowa, U. S. A.,[151] as long as every settler could obtain land, without increment of rent.   Such a commonwealth is, beyond all others, New Zealand, whose government favors with all its power the possession of small and middle-sized holdings of land, while at the same

time it narrows and dissolves, by all means at
its command the great landed properties, which
by the way, owing to lack of surplus laborers,
are almost incapable of producing rentals.[152]

In all these cases there is an astoundingly
equalized well-being, not perhaps mechanically
equal; but there is no wealth. *Because well-
being is the control over articles of consumption, while wealth is the dominion over
mankind.* In no such cases are the means of
production, "capital," "producing any surplus
values"; there are no "free laborers" and no
capitalism, and the political form of these communities approximates very closely to a "freemen's citizenship," and tends to approximate
it more and more, so far as the pressure of
the surrounding states, organized from and
based on the laws of war, permit its development. The "state" decomposes, or else in
new countries such as Utah or New Zealand,
it returns to a rudimentary stage of development; while the free self-determination of
free men, scarcely acquainted with a class fight,
constantly tends to pierce through ever more

thoroughly. Thus in the German Empire there was a parallel development between the political rise of the unions of the imperial free cities, the decline of the feudal states, the emancipation of the crafts, then still comprising the entire "plebs" of the cities, and the decay of the patrician control of the city government. This beneficent development was stopped by the erection of new primitive feudal states on the easterly border of the former German Empire, and thus the economic blossom of German culture was ruined. Whoever believes in a conscious purpose in history may say that the human race was again required to pass through another school of suffering before it could be redeemed. The Middle Ages had discovered the system of free labor, but had not developed it to its full capacity or efficiency. It was reserved for the new slavery of capitalism to discover and develop the incomparably more efficient system of coöperating labor, the division of labor in the workshops, in order to crown man as the ruler of natural forces, as king of the planet.

Slavery of antiquity and of modern capitalism was once necessary; now it has become superfluous. According to the story, every free citizen of Athens disposed of five human slaves; but we have supplied to our fellow citizens of modern society a vast mass of enslaved power, slaves of steel, that do not suffer in creating values. Since then we have ripened toward a civilization as much higher than the civilization of the time of Pericles, as the population, power and riches of the modern communities exceeds those of the tiny state of Athens.

Athens was doomed to dissolution—by reason of slavery as an economic institution, by reason of the political means. Having once entered that pathway, there was no outlet except death to the population. Our path will lead to life.

The same conclusion is found by either the historical-philosophical view, which took into account the tendency of the *development of the state,* or the study of political economy, which regards the tendency of *economic develop-*

ment; viz., that the economic means wins along
the whole line, while the political means disappears from the life of society, in that one of
its creations, which is most ancient and most
tenacious of life; capitalism decays with large
landed estates and ground rentals.

This has been the path of suffering and of
salvation of humanity, its Golgotha and its
resurrection into an eternal kingdom—from
war to peace, from the hostile splitting up of
the hordes to the peaceful unity of mankind,
from brutality to humanity, from the exploiting State of robbery to the Freemen's Citizenship.

NOTES

NOTES

1. "History is unable to demonstrate any one people, wherein the first traces of division of labor and of agriculture do not coincide with such agricultural exploitations, wherein the efforts of labor were not apportioned to one and the fruits of labor were not appropriated by some one else, wherein, in other words, the division of labor had not developed itself as the subjection of one set under the others."—Robertus-Jagetzow, *Illumination on the social question,* second edition. Berlin, 1890, p. 124. (Cf. *Immigration and Labor. The economic aspects of European Immigration to the United States,* by Dr. Isaac A. Hourwich. Putnam's, N. Y., 1912.— *Translator.*)

2. Achelis, *Die Ekstase in ihrer kulturellen Bedeutung,* vol. 1 of *Kulturprobleme der Gegenwart,* Berlin, 1902.

3. Grosse, *Formen der Familie.* Freiburg and Leipzig, 1896, p. 39.

4. Ratzel, *Völkerkunde.* Second Edition. Leipzig and Wien, 1894-5, II, p. 372.

5. *Die Soziale Verfassung des Inkareichs.* Stuttgart, 1896, p. 51.

6. *Siedlung und Agrarwesen der Westgermanen, etc.* Berlin, 1895, I, p. 273.

7. l. c. I, p. 138.

8. Ratzel, l. c. I, p. 702.

9. Ratzel, l. c. II, p. 555.

10. Ratzel, l. c. II, p. 555.

11. For example with the Ovambo according to Ratzel, l. c. II, p. 214, who in part "seem to be found in slave-like status," and according to Laveleye among the ancient Irish (*Fuidhirs*).

12. Ratzel, l. c. I, p. 648.

13. Ratzel, l. c. II, p. 99.

14. Lippert, *Kulturgeschichte der Menschheit*. Stuttgart, 1886, II, p. 302.

15. Lippert, l. c. II, p. 522.

16. *Römische Geschichte*. Sixth Edition. Berlin, 1874, I, p. 17.

17. Ratzel, l. c. II, p. 518.

18. Ratzel, l. c. I, p. 425.

19. Ratzel, l. c. II, p. 545.

20. Ratzel, l. c. II, pp. 390-1.

21. Ratzel, l. c. II, pp. 390-1.

22. Lippert, l. c. I, p. 471.

23. Kulischer, "The history of the development of interest from capital." *Jahrbücher für National Œkonomie*. III series, vol. 18, p. 318, Jena, 1899: (Says Strabo: "Plunderers and from the scant supplies of their native land covetous of the lands of others.")

24. Ratzel, l. c. I, p. 123.

25. Ratzel, l. c. I, p. 591.

26. Ratzel, l. c. II, p. 370.

27. Ratzel, l. c. II, pp. 390-1.

28. Ratzel, l. c. II, pp. 388-9.

29. Ratzel, l. c. II, pp. 103-04.

30. Thurnwald, *Staat und Wirtschaft im altem Ægypten. Zeitschrift für Soz. Wissenchaft*, vol. 4 1901, pp. 700-01.

81. Ratzel, l. c. II, pp. 404-05. (Gumplowicz, *Rassenkampf,* p. 264: "Egypt, rich and self-sufficient, says Ranke, invited the avarice of neighboring tribes, who served other gods. Under the name of the Shepherd peoples, foreign dynasts and foreign tribes ruled Egypt for centuries.

"Truly, the summary of universal history could not be begun with more characteristic words than those of Ranke. For in the words applied to Egypt the quintessence of the whole history of mankind is summed up."— *Translator.*)

32. Ratzel, l. c. II, p. 165.

33. Ratzel, l. c. II, p. 485.

34. Ratzel, l. c. II, p. 480.

35. Ratzel, l. c. II, p. 165.

36. Buhl, *Soziale Verhältnisse der Israeliten,* p. 13.

37. Ratzel, l. c. II, p. 455.

38. Ratzel, l. c. I, p. 628.

39. Ratzel, l. c. I, p. 625.

40. Cieza de Leon, "Seg. parte de la crónica del Peru." P. 75, cit. by Cunow, *Inkareich* (p. 62, note 1).

41. Cunow, l. c. p. 61.

42. Ratzel, l. c. II, p. 346.

43. Ratzel, l. c. II, pp. 36-7.

44. Ratzel, l. c. II, p. 221. (Cf. remarks by Hon. A. J. Sabath, M. C., *Sociological Argument on Workman's Compensation Bill,* p. 498, Senate Document 338, Sixty-second Congress, Second Session, Volume I. See also *Congressional Record* for March 1, 1913, Sixty-second Congress, Third Session, pp. 4503, 4529, *et seq.—Translator.*)

45. "Among the Wahuma women occupy a higher posi-

tion than among the negroes, and are watched carefully by their men. This makes mixed marriages difficult. The mass of the Waganda even to-day would not have remained a genuine negro tribe 'of dark chocolate colored skin and short wool hair' were it not that the two peoples are strictly opposed to one another as peasants and herdsmen, rulers and subjects, as despised and honored, in spite of the relations entered into among the upper classes. In this peculiar position, they represent a typical phenomenon, which is found repeated at many other points."—Ratzel, l. c. II, p. 177.

46. Ratzel, l. c. II, p. 178.

47. Ratzel, l. c. II, p. 198.

48. Ratzel, l. c. II, p. 476.

49. Ratzel, l. c. II, p. 453.

50. Kopp, *Griechische Staatsaltertümer*, 2, *Aufl.* Berlin, 1893, p. 23.

51. Uhland, *Alte hoch und niederdeutsche Volkslieder* I (1844), p. 339 cited by Sombart: *Der moderne Kapitalismus*, Leipzig, 1902, I, pp. 384-5.

52. Inama-Sternegg, *Deutsche Wirtsch.-Gesch.* I, Leipzig, 1879, p. 59.

53. Westermarck, *History of Human Marriage*, London, 1891, p. 368.

54. Cf. Ratzel, l. c. I, p. 81.

55. Ratzel, l. c. I, p. 156.

56. Ratzel, l. c. I, pp. 259-60.

57. Ratzel, l. c. II, p. 434.

58. I. Kulischer, l. c., p. 317, where other examples may be found.

59. Westermarck, *History of Human Marriage*, p.

400, which contains a number of ethnographical examples.

60. Westermarck, l. c., p. 546.

61. Cf. Ratzel, l. c. I, pp. 318, 540.

62. Ratzel, l. c. I, p. 106.

63. Ratzel, l. c. I, p. 335.

64. Ratzel, l. c. I, p. 346.

65. Ratzel, l. c. I, p. 347.

66. Buecher, *Entstehung der Volkswirtschaft,* Second Edition, Tübingen, 1898, p. 301.

67. Cf., Ratzel, l. c. I, p. 271, speaking of the islanders of the Pacific Ocean: "Intercourse from tribe to tribe is carried on by inviolable heralds, preferably old women. These act also as intermediary agents in trades." See also page 317 for the same practises among the Australians.

68. German Translation by L. Katscher. Leipzig, 1907.

69. Ratzel, l. c. I, p. 81.

70. Ratzel, l. c. I, pp. 478-9.

71. A. Vierkandt, *Die wirtschaftlichen Verhältnisse der Naturvölker. Zeitschrift für Sozialwissenschaft,* II, pp. 177-8.

72. Kulischer, l. c. pp. 320-1.

73. Lippert, l. c. I, p. 266, *et seq.*

74. Cf. Westermarck, *History of Human Marriage.*

75. Ratzel, l. c. II, p. 27.

76. Herodotus IV, 23, cited by Lippert, l. c. I, p. 459.

77. Lippert, l. c. II, p. 170.

78. Mommsen, l. c. I, p. 139.

79. Similar conditions may be observed among the

islanders near India. Here the Malays are vikings. "Colonization is an important factor, as conquest and settlement oversea . . . reminding one of the great rôle played in ancient Hellas by the roving tribes. . . . Every strip of coast line shows foreign elements, who enter uncalled for and in most instances spreading damage among the natives. The right of conquest was granted by the rulers of Tornate to noble dynasts, who later on became semi-sovereign viceroys on the islands of Buru, Serang, etc."

80. Mommsen, l. c. I, p. 132.
81. Mommsen, l. c. I, p. 134.
82. Ratzel, l. c. I, p. 160.
83. Ratzel, l. c. II, p. 558.
84. Buhl, l. c., p. 48.
85. Buhl, l. c., pp. 78-79.
86. Mommsen, l. c. II, p. 406.
87. Ratzel, l. c. II, p. 191; cf. also pp. 207-8.
88. Ratzel, l. c. I, p. 363.
89. Mommsen, l. c., p. 46.
90. Both cited by Kulischer, l. c., p. 319, from: Buechsenschuetz, *Besitz und Erwerb im griechischen Altertum;* and Goldschmidt, *History of the Law of Commerce.*
91. Ratzel, l. c. I, p. 263.
92. F. Oppenheimer's *Grossgrundeigentum und soziale Frage.* Book Two, Chapter I. Berlin, 1898.
93. Nomadism is exceptionally characterized by the facility with which, from patriarchal conditions, despotic functions are developed with most far-reaching powers. Ratzel, l. c. Vol. II, pp. 388-9.
94. Ratzel, l. c. I, p. 408.

95. Cunow, l. c. pp. 66-7. Similarly among the inhabitants of the Malay Islands numerous examples are found in Radak (Ratzel, l. c. I, p. 267).

96. Buhl, l. c., p. 17.

97. Ratzel, l. c. II, p. 66.

98. Ratzel, l. c. II, p. 118.

99. Ratzel, l. c. II, p. 167.

100. Ratzel, l. c. II, p. 218.

101. Ratzel, l. c. I, p. 125.

102. Ratzel, l. c. I, p. 124.

103. Ratzel, l. c. I, p. 118.

104. Ratzel, l. c. I, p. 125.

105. Ratzel, l. c. I, p. 346.

106. Ratzel, l. c. II, p. 245.

107. Ratzel, l. c. I, pp. 267-8.

108. Mommsen, l. c. III, pp. 234-5.

109. Ratzel, l. c. II, p. 167.

110. Ratzel, l. c. II, p. 229.

111. Ratzel, l. c. I, p. 128.

112. Weber's *Weltgeschichte*, III, p. 163.

113. Thurnwald, l. c., pp. 702-3.

114. Thurnwald, l. c., p. 712; cf. Schneider, *Kultur und Denken der alten Ægypter*, Leipzig, 1907, p. 38.

115. Ratzel, l. c. II, p. 599.

116. Ratzel, l. c. II, p. 362.

117. Ratzel, l. c. II, p. 344.

118. Meitzen, l. c. II, p. 633.

119. Inama-Sternegg, l. c. I, pp. 140-1.

120. Mommsen, l. c. V, p. 84.

121. Cf. the detailed exposition of this in F. Oppenheimer's *Grossgrundeigentum und die soziale Frage*, Book II, Chap. 3.

122. Mommsen, l. c. III, pp. 234-5.

123. Thurnwald, l. c., p. 771.

124. Meitzen, l. c. I, pp. 362f.

125. Inama-Sternegg, l. c. I, pp. 373, 386.

126. Cf. F. Oppenheimer's *Grossgrundeigentum*, p. 272.

127. Thurnwald, l. c., p. 706.

128. Ratzel, l. c. II, p. 503.

129. Ratzel, l. c. II, p. 518.

130. Meitzen, l. c. I, p. 579: "At the time of the compilation of the Lex Salica, the ancient racial nobility had been reduced to common freemen or else had been annihilated. The officials, on the other hand, are rated at threefold wergeld, 600 solidi, and if one be *'puer regis'* 300 solidi."

131. Thurnwald, l. c. p. 712.

132. Inama-Sternegg, l. c. II, p. 61.

133. Thurnwald, l. c., p. 705.

134. "The larger camps of the army of the Rhine obtained their municipal annexes partly through army suttlers and camp followers, and particularly through the veterans, who after the completion of their services remained in their accustomed quarters. Thus there arose distinct from the military quarters proper, a distinct town of cabins (*Canabæ*). In all parts of the Empire, and especially in the various Germanias, there arose in the course of time, from these camps of the legionaries, and particularly from the headquarter stations, cities in the modern sense."—Mommsen, l. c. V, p. 153.

135. Eisenhardt, *Gesch. der National Oekonomie*, p. 9: "Aided by the new and more liquid means of pay-

ment in cash, it became possible to call into being a new and more independent establishment of soldiers and of officials. As they were paid only periodically it became impossible for them to make themselves independent (as the feudatories had done) and then to turn on their paymaster."

136. Thurnwald, l. c., p. 773.

137. Thurnwald, l. c., p. 699.

138. Thurnwald, l. c., p. 709.

139. Thurnwald, l. c., p. 711.

140. Cf. with this F. Oppenheimer's *Grossgrundeigentum etc.*, Book II, Chap. 3.

141. "Tendency, i. e., a law, whose absolute execution is checked by countervailing circumstances, or is by them retarded, or weakened." Marx, *Kapital*, vol. III, p. 215.

142. Cf. the excellent work of Peter Kropotkin, *Mutual Aid in its Development*.

143. Cf. F. Oppenheimer, *Die Siedlungsgenossenschaft etc.*, Berlin, 1896, and his *Grossgrundeigentum und soziale Frage*, Berlin, 1898.

144. Cf. F. Oppenheimer, *Bevölkerungsgesetz des T. R. Malthus. Darstellung und Kritik*, Berlin–Bern, 1901.

145. Cf. F. Oppenheimer, *Grundgesetz der Marxschen Gesellschaftslehre, Darstellung und Kritik*, Berlin, 1903.

146. Cf. F. Oppenheimer, *Grundgesetz der Marxschen Gesellschaftslehre*, Part IV., particularly, the twelfth chapter: "Tendency of the Capitalistic Development."

147. Cf. F. Oppenheimer, *Grossgrundeigentum und soziale Frage, Berlin*, 1898. Book I, Chapter 2, Section 3, "Philosophy of the Social Body," pp. 57 *et seq.*

148. Cf. F. Oppenheimer, *Grossgrundeigentum*, Book II, Chap. 2, Sec. 3, p. 322.

149. Cf. F. Oppenheimer, *Grossgrundeigentum*, Book II, Chap. 3, Sec. 4, especially pp. 423 *et seq.*

150. Cf. F. Oppenheimer, "Die Utopie als Tatsache," *Zeitschrift für Sozial-Wissenschaft*, 1899, Vol. II, pp. 190 *et seq.*

151. Cf. F. Oppenheimer, *Siedlungsgenossenschaft*, pp. 477 *et seq.*

152. Cf. André Siegfried, *La démocratie en Nouvelle Zelande*, Paris, 1904.